Raising Black Children
Who Love
Reading and Writing

Raising Black Children Who Love Reading and Writing

A Guide from Birth Through Grade Six

Dierdre Glenn Paul
Foreword by Catherine Dorsey-Gaines

3/01

BERGIN & GARVEY
Westport, Connecticut • London

Library of Congress Cataloging-in-Publication Data

Paul, Dierdre Glenn, 1964–
    Raising Black children who love reading and writing : a guide from birth through grade six / Dierdre Glenn Paul ; foreword by Catherine Dorsey-Gaines.
        p.   cm.
    Includes bibliographical references (p.   ) and index.
    ISBN 0–89789–555–X (alk. paper)
    1. Afro-Americans—Education (Elementary)   2. Afro-Americans—Education (Early childhood)   3. Language arts (Elementary)—United States.   4. Language arts (Early childhood)—United States.
    I. Title.
    LC2778.L34P28   2000
    649′.58—dc21   99–40490

British Library Cataloguing in Publication Data is available.

Library of Congress Catalog Card Number: 99–40490
ISBN: 0–89789–555–X

First published in 2000

Bergin & Garvey, 88 Post Road West, Westport, CT 06881
An imprint of Greenwood Publishing Group, Inc.
www.greenwood.com

Printed in the United States of America

The paper used in this book complies with the Permanent Paper Standard issued by the National Information Standards Organization (Z39.48–1984).

10 9 8 7 6 5 4 3 2 1

To my daughter, Z., and newly arrived son, C.
—My future

I searched hard and, in one book or another, I found them [black writers and heroes] waiting for me with fire in their tongues, speaking a language that bolstered my hopes. I listened. Plainly Richard Wright was telling me that a great shadow was moving steadily across the land; that the spirit of the black man was in that shadow—moving it along. Other black writers and poets emerged, fulfilling Wright's words. Langston Hughes, W.E.B. Du Bois and Arna Bontemps moved in to expand my vision. Then came Ralph Ellison, speaking of the invisibility of blacks in the eyes of whites, and James Baldwin, warning me about *The Fire Next Time*. Before long I was neck deep in black literature. Indeed, it was a pleasant surprise to learn that black blood flowed in the veins of Alexander Pushkin, Russia's famed poet.

—Gordon Parks, Photographer/Filmmaker
(as quoted in the introduction of Archie Given's
*Spirited Minds: African American Books
for Our Brothers and Sons*)

Contents

Contents

Foreword

Raising Black Children Who Love Reading and Writing: A Guide from Birth Through Grade Six begins with a historical perspective noting that African Americans have had an interesting and complex relationship with language since their forcible transport from Africa to the United States between 1619 and 1858. Slave masters, after arriving in the United States, determined this relationship because of their insecurity concerning whether slaves should be educated.

Dierdre Glenn Paul has taken this parent's/caregiver's guide and elevated it to the level of an important and powerful work. This work, which is designated for use by parents and caregivers, I believe is equally as important for classroom teachers, administrators, and community personnel.

Paul sets reading and writing within the context of Black enslavement in the United States. At one time, the price of exercising such skills by Blacks often precipitated punishment or possible death at the hands of the White master. This historical framework gives the reader the idea that no matter how offensive these laws were against reading and writing, the enslaved took deliberate chances in order to increase his or her desire to understand the written word. With this legacy, parents and caregivers who raise Black children to love reading and writing will know that a firm foundation has been planted.

Dierdre Glenn Paul incorporates herself into this work by becoming a part of the reader's psyche, by knowing the affective way the reader will relate to this work. She puts herself into the emotional as well as the intellectual confines of the reader. This establishes with the parent/caregiver an understanding of what it takes to bridge the emotional and social responses of children in order for them to learn to read and write. But this is just the skeleton of the work. It is the complex energies, social understanding, and emotional interactions with the written word that will help the child become not only a reader and writer of words but one who will be a lover of the written word for a lifetime.

As I read the "guide," I was particularly impressed by the way Paul articulates the theoretical and practical experiences of linguists, educators, reading specialists, and researchers. This gives impetus to the academic searching of professional resources. However, the beauty of this work is not only its step-by-step process, which helps the parent/caregiver in nurturing the child to become a reader and writer, but the knowledge given to the reader of the why, how, and when of the difficult process of becoming literate.

This book reinforces the idea that a literate society is not a society of privilege for one ethnic group but a literate society for all. It matters not the economic status or political status of people, the attainment of literacy is a goal for all members of our American society. Later, however, some of us find out that literacy is not always liberating, and these folk become disillusioned with the educative process.

In the foreword of the book *Growing Up Literate: Learning from Inner City Families* by Denny Taylor and me, Rudine Sims Bishop quotes James Baldwin in an interview in the *New York Times Book Review* (September 23, 1979). It seems appropriate to repeat it here:

> The bottom line is this: You write in order to change the world, knowing perfectly well that you probably can't. . . . In some way, your aspirations and concern for a single man in fact do begin to change the world. The world changes according to the way people see it, and if you alter, even by a millimeter, the way a person or people look at reality, then you can change it.

Dierdre Glenn Paul has approached the writing of this "guide" with a simple pen and paper technique and has produced a much needed work for her intended audience. It has great possibility for reaching a broader audience—an audience that is thirsty for the knowledge that this young woman has written for black children but is valuable for all children in these United States. Additional evidence of the prospect of a broader reach is the college professor of reading and language arts. In the dedication of this book, Dierdre Glenn Paul presents this work to her progeny. As I read her work, I found it a legacy to my children as well; children who [now] are struggling parents with a desire to make their children lifelong lovers of reading and writing. Because of this important, powerful work, I know my children's task will be made easier.

Catherine Dorsey-Gaines

Acknowledgments

It is absurd to assume, as has been the tendency among a great many Western anthropologists and sociologists, that all traces of Africa were erased from the Negro's mind because he learned English. The very nature of the English the Negro spoke and still speaks drops the lie on that idea.

—Amiri Baraka (LeRoi Jones), Poet

Writing my first nonfiction book has proved to be, concomitantly, one of the most rewarding and challenging experiences that I have had. The process of bringing this project from dream to fruition was complicated by life's vicissitudes: parenting a two-year-old, undergoing a second pregnancy, teaching full-time, giving birth, sustaining divorce, and operating on very little sleep. Yet, I would relinquish none of these adventures. They have all added to the quality of my life, while simultaneously teaching me and extending my boundaries.

It is my hope that this book will be received in the spirit in which it was written, a spirit of love, understanding, and compassion. Although joyous, parenting is one of the most difficult tasks that may be experienced in life. It is my desire to help other parents and caregivers in lightening the load and enhancing the satisfaction gained.

Yet, this book would never have reached completion without the encouragement, support, and assistance of many different people and entities. I would like to personally thank the Montclair State University Alumni Association, the MSU College of Education and Human Services, and the Office of Research and Sponsored Programs for providing me with grants that aided in the book's completion.

I would like to thank Dean Nicholas Michelli for his belief in my work and encouragement, affirming that I have something of value to share.

I thank Dr. D. Joy Stone, Reading and Educational Media Chairperson, for her attempts to guide and teach me. Although it might not have always appeared so, they have been greatly appreciated.

I thank Khafre Abif, Gloria Chuff, Nancy Crowley, Annette Dade, and Dana Prokopiak for their guidance, camaraderie, and willingness to read so many children's and adolescent books, in addition to writing the annotations contained within Appendix A. Thanks also for good talk during our discussion groups and after meetings in my office.

I thank Dr. Catherine Dorsey-Gaines for her eagerness to coach me through this process. I thank Dr. Dorothy Strickland for introducing me to Dr. Dorsey-Gaines. Most significantly, I thank them both for the examples that they have provided, the significant contributions to literacy education and Black scholarship they have made, and their sincere desire to help young Black scholars along the way. They actualize the proverb of *each one, teach[ing] one.*

I thank Dr. Violet Harris for her patience, straight talk, and desire to see me succeed; in addition, she has helped to inspire a love for multicultural children's literature.

I thank Donna Barkman for exposing me to the vast and exciting world of children's and adolescent literature.

I thank Tina Jacobowitz for her tremendous belief in my capabilities, her candor, and loving friendship.

I thank Wandalyn Enix for her friendship and desire to see me always strive for excellence.

I would also like to thank those at Greenwood who have helped this book reach print. I thank Jane Garry for giving me a first chance. I thank Marcia Goldstein and Heidi Straight for their regular communications with me and tremendous attention to detail.

I thank Andrea Wilks, and the staff of Bank Street Book Store, for pinpointing books that I might wish to review and include, providing quick analyses, and shipping books to me expediently.

I thank the staff of the Englewood Library for their assistance, in respect to information checks.

Quite significantly, I would like to thank my sister, Aliya, and my mother, Carolyn, for carrying a large portion of my load as I attempted to juggle the responsibilities of parenting, home, teaching, and writing.

Lastly, I thank my children for allowing me the freedom to vigorously pursue dreams.

Chapter 1

Introduction

African Americans have, historically, had a complex and distinctive relationship with language and literacy within the borders of the United States. During the Middle Passage (defined, in this instance, as the forcible transport of slaves by ship, legally and illegally, from Africa to the United States between the years 1619–1858), enslaved Africans lost attributes associated with African language and culture that had a devastating effect on their sense of identity and self-esteem.

TRANSITION AND ORALITY

In all probability, the enslaved spoke Ibo, Hausa, Mende, Yoruban, and other West and West-Central African languages. On arrival, however, they struggled to grasp the unfamiliar oral language of their masters, overseers, and even fellow slaves. It was a common practice of enslavers to mix different tribes of Africans within slave communities, in an effort to minimize the chances of revolt and increase the sense of isolation slaves felt.

In spite of these challenges, however, African Americans learned to use oral language in ways that bridged aspects of their native tongues with Standard American and British English. The enslaved developed an English pidgin that served as the language of transaction between Whites and themselves, as well as *among* themselves in some instances. Eventually, this pidgin evolved into a Creole (English words were substituted for West and West-Central African ones, while the idiom and structure remained consistent with West and West-Central African linguistic patterns).

With time, these involuntary immigrants even learned to use a codified English that directly conveyed the speaker's message to fellow Blacks, while appearing inconsequential and benign to Euro-American listeners. In a similar sense, important precepts and lessons about survival under the racist and oppressive institution of slavery were passed from one generation of slaves to the next through proverbs, folklore, folktales, naming practices, narratives, and song. Many of these tales and songs could be directly traced to Africa. Approximately 65% of the folktales told by slaves in the 19th-century American South were specifically linked to Africa.

Clandestine codes and origin, however, were sometimes missed by Euro-American compilers, such as Joel Chandler Harris, who capitalized on their mass market proliferation. For example, the character Brer Rabbit was symbolic of the slave and representative of hope. Each time Brer Rabbit outwitted his physically larger and more powerful opponent, the slave had cause to celebrate. If it was possible for Brer Rabbit, it was possible for the slave to break the bonds of domination.

One outcome of the unique and difficult linguistic journey that African Americans have traveled has been a highly stylized and linguistically sophisticated Black English Vernacular that features a characteristic grammar and pronunciation, in addition to differentiating verbal rituals and vocabulary.

According to linguist Geneva Smitherman, in her book *Talkin and Testifyin: The Language of Black America*, some of the rituals include: (1) call and response patterns (spontaneous verbal and nonverbal interactions between speaker and listener in which all of the speaker's utterances are punctuated by expressions from the listener); (2) signification (the act of talking negatively about someone through cunning verbal insults); and (3) tonal semantics (the use of voice rhythm and vocal inflection to convey meaning).

Yet, most significantly, African Americans acquired literacy, in spite of perilous consequences.

A LONG AND PERILOUS JOURNEY— THE ACQUISITION OF LITERACY

The institution of slavery produced a number of dilemmas for enslavers, among them the issue of whether the enslaved should be educated. Oppositional factions of slave owners debated the need for education among slaves. Some believed that education would make the enslaved more "governable," and others believed that education would have a deleterious effect.

The debate's outcome was that the enslaved were prohibited (by law) from learning to read and write in many regions of the pre–Civil War South. There was a strong correlation between the enactment of such laws, a series of slave insurrections, and the proliferation of abolitionist pamphlets and tracts.

Slaves' acquisition of literacy, the ability and willingness to use reading and writing to construct meaning from printed text, was considered a capital offense in a number of states.

For the enslaved, literacy often served as a first step in breaking the psychological and physical fetters of slavery. In his autobiography *Life and Times of Frederick Douglass*, former slave Frederick Douglass discussed the transformative effects of literacy on his life:

> And as I read, behold! the very discontent so graphically predicted by Master Hugh had already come upon me. I was no longer the light-hearted, gleesome boy, full of mirth and play, . . . Light had penetrated the moral dungeon where I had lain, and I saw the bloody whip for my back, and the iron chain for my feet, and my "good, kind" master, he was the author of my situation.

The written word provided Douglass with his first vision of "freedom" and led to his decision to seek his physical emancipation from slavery.

For the free Black (since all Blacks of this time were not slaves), literacy was an influential signifier, especially since free Blacks' access to educational opportunity was severely restricted because of both custom and law.

In contemporary society, literacy has freed many from chains that aren't as tangible as those of slavery. Poet and author Maya Angelou, in her autobiography *I Know Why the Caged Bird Sings*, wrote of the way in which the love of reading and books helped her survive a childhood rape and the subsequent murder of her rapist. Angelou expressed her belief that she had caused the death of her attacker with her words. Resultantly, she stopped speaking. The beauty of literature and a kind and loving mentor who shared Angelou's love of books gave her back her voice.

Within the African American community, literacy had proved emancipatory and empowering, as well as entertaining. In consideration of our rich and multidimensional history with words in the United States, it is difficult for me to reconcile that a people who mastered language and literacy under such abysmal circumstances have produced a generation of children who are unable to grasp these concepts sufficiently in present-day society. At least, this is the portrayal widely disseminated about us.

A GENERATION WITHOUT HOPE?

Our children's failure is often attributed to their own personal shortcomings, in addition to those of their parents, communities, and teachers. This view is routinely presented by the media and alarmist governmental reports. In my estimation, blame would be more properly assigned to school systems, political bureaucracies, and societal inequity. This outlook regarding a more precise assignment of culpability has been informed by the work of educational researchers and theorists, such as Carter G. Woodson, James Banks, Henry Giroux, Jonathan Kozol, and Ira Shor, as well as my own personal observations.

If the current, mainstream assessment of our children and our concern for their educational progress is examined within a historical framework, it is incongruent. First of all, the long-term denial of education in the antebellum South instilled a deep respect and passionate longing for it within Black communities. There were always the realizations that knowledge equaled power and that the first step in the systematic denigration of a people began with the denial of education and literacy.

Ninety-five percent of African Americans were left without the ability to read and write by the end of the Civil War. With the advent of Reconstruction (1863–1877) and the demise of slavery, the government instituted the Freedman's Bureau in 1865. One of the Bureau's primary responsibilities was to supervise schooling for recently emancipated Blacks. Black schools (at all educational levels) were initiated. During the years 1867–1872, the Bureau chartered day schools, night schools, and trade schools. These schools were often reliant on the financial gifts of White benefactors and philanthropists, even though there were concerns among some Blacks that such contributions would make them once again dependent on Whites.

The concern regarding renewed dependence sparked the establishment of Black schools, founded and financially sustained by formerly enslaved Blacks. Black church-operated "Sabbath schools," which provided literacy instruction during evenings and weekends, were also instituted for those who were unable to attend school during the day.

These events speak volumes to the heartfelt sentiment among Blacks that education and literacy were valuable commodities.

Further, the Reconstruction-era struggle for education among Blacks served as a precedent in the historical battle endured by them for education, generally, and equal education, more specifically.

Traditionally, the Black church and family (nuclear and extended) have considered language learning of prime importance. Reading the Bible and Sunday school materials, recitations, holiday speeches, and pageant participation were mainstays for Black children routinely attending church. In Black communities, children often heard and participated in family discussions, read and wrote letters for their elders, and "talk" permeated their environments.

My experience with the numbers of Black children I have taught within the past 13 years tells me that many are continuing to have such experiences with language and literacy. I have frequently encountered Black children who still hold intense and joyful conversations with their peers and families, perform in church pageants, recite rap and song from memory, and write marvelous, creative tales, journal entries, and poems.

However, I have also heard these children express tremendous dissatisfaction with the school system, the curriculum, and the reading materials with which they are presented. What causes children, who love using language and literacy for their own purposes, to abhor the way it is taught in school?

These are the types of questions that parents with whom I come in contact ask. There is a genuine sense of bewilderment for many and a sincere desire to help their children. I routinely meet parents (of all income groups) who realize that literacy *remains* emancipatory and empowering. In many ways, it ensures Black survival and success. Historically, it has provided Blacks with the only true means of class mobility. Today, it provides children with enhanced options in a society that regularly denies access to those who are perceived as not using language and literacy with facility.

It should also be noted that some parents wonder whether the teachers are the culprits in this matter. I wish it were as simple to draw enemy lines.

As a current teacher educator, I would state that the problem is more complex in nature. Many of the teachers with whom I have worked have a sincere interest in helping children. In some instances, teachers are simply unable to do so.

Generally, large numbers of teachers work under harsh conditions, which include low per-pupil expenditure, crumbling facilities, appallingly poor pay, and insufficient or inappropriate opportunities for staff development. There will be a more comprehensive discussion of the issues that plague modern school systems, Black children, and teachers in the next chapter.

In respect to issues of racial and ethnic diversity, there is a lack of awareness and knowledge on the part of some Euro-American teachers about the ways in which children of color can best be served.

Teachers of color comprise less than 15% of the teaching force and less than 12% of school administrators. Black teachers comprise about 6.9% of the teaching force, and they are projected to comprise less than 5% by the year 2000.

In reference to such a projection, one researcher (as quoted in Jacqueline Jordan Irvine's *Black Students and School Failure: Policies, Practices, and Prescriptions*) has characterized the situation in the following fashion: "A minority teaching force of this size would mean that the average student, who has about 40 teachers during his precollegiate years (grades K–12), can expect at best to encounter only two teachers who are members of a minority group during his entire school career."

But, teachers of color are often called on to serve as role models, culture brokers, and advocates, in addition to teaching. The term *culture broker* is defined, by educational researcher Geneva Gay in her article "Building Cultural Bridges: A Bold Proposal for Teacher Education," as "one who thoroughly understands different cultural systems, is able to interpret cultural symbols . . . mediate cultural incompatibilities, and . . . establish linkages across cultures that facilitate the instructional process."

Further, while many parents and teachers are committed to children's academic success and development, there are those who cannot or will not devote such effort.

It is my hope that *Raising Black Children Who Love Reading and Writing: A Guide from Birth Through Grade Six* will serve as a resource for Black parents, interracial couples with Black children, adoptive and foster parents of Black children, as well as teachers and other school professionals who are committed to and concerned about literacy development.

This book will examine particular themes that are associated with the enhancement of language and literacy skills in Black children (from infancy to grade six). The book seeks to provide concrete suggestions and an annotated bibliography of children's and adolescent literature that will assist you in your efforts to raise Black children who love reading.

Traditionally, issues surrounding child development and parent education have been cast in a light that is supposedly apolitical and neutral.

In actuality, they have been quite political and partisan in their attempts to characterize mainstream values and concerns as the norm and other perspectives as unenlightened and extremist.

Within the context of this book, I do not make such claims. This book is, decidedly, political and representative of a distinctive stance on Blackness, education, and literacy.

Although I do not pretend to have all the answers, I believe the benefit of my experiences (both as an educator and a parent) and my trained expertise will help you in making the best choices for your children.

NOTE

The reader might have noticed my seemingly interchangeable use of the terms "Black" and "African American" in this discussion. In most instances, I use the descriptors quite consciously. When I use "Black," I do so in an attempt to express the deep connection among all of the African Diaspora. I do not suggest that there is a monolith of the Black experience. I realize that there are both individual and class-based distinctions that should be considered. Additionally, this book is meant to include children and their families who have recently migrated from Africa, the Caribbean, and South America. Thus, it will feature stories from their experience as well.

Chapter 2

Black Child/U.S. School System

Education remains the key to both economic and political empowerment.
—Barbara Jordan, Educator and former Congresswoman
(as quoted in Tamara Nikuradse's *My Mother Had a Dream: African-American Women Share Their Mothers' Words of Wisdom*)

Although the American educational system has its problems, there are reasons for optimism. Yes, such reasons exist, even for children of color and the poor. Although educational progress for *all* children remains a dream to strive toward, the situation is not as bleak as we are often led to believe. In this chapter, we will commence by sharing the successes of an institution that both serves as an easy target and is used as a scapegoat by the press and politicians.

GOOD NEWS

In many ways, we (as a society) engage in a nostalgia that romanticizes the past. We talk about the good old days frequently. For some, the talk includes notions that teachers cared more because they came from within the community and we learned more. In her book *Teaching to Transgress*, scholar and public intellectual bell hooks talks about her teachers within a segregated school system in the following manner:

Almost all of our teachers . . . were black women. They were committed to nurturing intellect so that we could become scholars, thinkers, and cultural workers—black folks who used our "minds." We learned that our devotion to learning, to a life of the mind, was a counter-hegemonic act, a fundamental way to resist every strategy of white racist colonization.

At that point in time, teaching was considered one of the few leadership positions available to women within the Black community. Also, Black teachers were more apt to be hired and retained in segregated school systems. These factors, however, do not detract from these teachers' commitment nor minimize their comprehensive understanding that "teaching Black children is a revolutionary act," according to acclaimed author and activist James Baldwin (as quoted in Michele Foster's *Black Teachers on Teaching*).

While there is no doubt that Black teachers played influential roles in the development of Black children and communities, hooks fails to explicitly state that the impact that those teachers had on her has manifested itself in a generation of Black teachers and scholars who are carrying on the tradition and improving it in numerous ways. Although their current numbers may be small, they are affecting the lives of more children and young people than their predecessors had, as a result of Civil Rights–era gains.

It should also be noted that although education for Blacks within a segregated school system may have been positive for some children because of the nurturing pedagogy of and devotion shared by their teachers, the unequal distribution of funding and opportunity doomed Black schools and many Black children within them to failure. Within the walls of the allegedly "separate but equal" Black schools of the segregated South, there were extreme supply shortages; children were compelled to use the cast-off, dilapidated books of their White counterparts; and school buildings were often unfit for occupancy.

In many ways, this description is still applicable. Within sectors of our contemporary school system (especially urban centers and rural areas), de facto segregation has replaced the de jure segregation that preceded the 1954 *Brown vs. Topeka Board of Education* ruling. Yet, there has been positive change as well. There are currently more educators, of all races and ethnicities, who are involved in systematic efforts to improve education for all children.

Curriculum specialists are making greater efforts to develop curriculums that are multicultural, historically accurate, and reflective of the pluralistic society in which we live. Yet, such attempts to improve schooling for all students are often politicized. In some instances, the politicization has had serious consequences for the curricular reform recommended or for those who have spearheaded it.

For example, the *African American Baseline Essays*, edited by Asa Hilliard and Carolyn Leonard in 1990, is one of the most widely used Afrocentric teacher resources in the United States. The essays (originally developed for the Portland, Oregon, school system) are divided into six separate components, each detailing Black achievements in language arts, art, mathematics, history, music, and science. Although the essays are attempts to revise flawed history, make significant the cultural contributions of Blacks, and raise the self-esteem of Black children, they have been maligned in the press as inaccurate and misleading. The scholars affiliated with the essays' development have had their credentials and motives questioned.

Similar criticisms were made about suggested curriculum reforms in New York City and New York State. Both *A Curriculum of Inclusion* and *One Nation, Many Peoples: A Declaration of Cultural Interdependence* (reports commissioned by the New York State Board of Regents) were placed under intense scrutiny for attempting to rewrite history; giving Blacks, Latinos, Asians, and Native Americans a central role in the telling of history; and interrogating the ethics of Eurocentric conquest and heroism.

Those involved in these projects (such as Professor Leonard Jeffries) were suddenly cast into the harsh gaze of the public eye, tried in the media, and found "racist." Although some of Dr. Jeffries's comments have been questionable and could be considered in poor taste, it appears odd that he was vilified only after suggesting revisions to curriculum taught in public schools.

In spite of such attacks, however, curricular reform efforts still move forward. Greater numbers of teachers are using innovative classroom approaches to meet the instructional needs of the children in their charge. They are using multicultural materials and curriculum models, as well as interdisciplinary methods that show students the varied connections between content areas such as language arts, mathematics, and social studies.

More children's and adolescent literature is used in classrooms in an effort to make learning relevant to students' lives and personal needs. Manipulatives and real-life applications are being utilized to make mathematics more easily comprehensible to students.

In respect to satisfying students' personal needs, there are large numbers of teachers who volunteer to supervise free breakfast and after-school programs; provide students with tutoring during the hour before school begins or during their lunch periods; take students, who might not receive the opportunity otherwise, on college visits; and speak to parents on behalf of children who cannot.

Relatedly, there are more quality teacher education programs producing teachers who are prepared to nurture students and cope with issues of diversity. We all know, however, that we still have a long way to go. Nationally, TEPs (Teacher Education Programs) are equipping numbers of Euro-American students to demonstrate cultural awareness and sensitivity, in addition to pedagogical skill. Simultaneously, these programs are seeking to *recruit* and *retain* students of color.

Recruitment and retention are difficult tasks for a myriad of reasons. Students of color now have more professional and profitable options available to them than their ancestors had. Many do not view the field of education with the same respect that it once garnered in communities of color. Also, students of color are not attending college in record numbers. Sometimes, they are academically underprepared and tracked in the school systems they have attended. In too many instances, Native American, Latino, and Black students are dropping out of school.

Yet, there has been some progress for Black students in this respect. Statistics show that there has been an increase in the median years of schooling completed by Black students from 8.0 years in 1970 to 12.0 in 1985. But this statistic does not reflect whether these students exit schools with diplomas and certificates.

There have also been educational gains related to testing for Black students. According to the National Assessment of Educational Progress (NAEP), one of the most comprehensive surveys of achievement, nine-year-old Black students increased their average reading proficiency scores by 7.2 points between 1975–1988, while Black 13-year-olds made a 17.2 point gain and 17-year-olds increased their scores by 34 points. The NAEP, insituted during the 1970s by the federal government, was designed to serve as a periodic monitor of U.S. students' achievement in reading and other academic content area subjects. The NAEP usually tests each four years and has traditionally summarized data for 9-, 14- and 17-year-olds.

As I present these test scores, however, I feel uncomfortable and I am reminded of the famous quote, "there are lies, damn lies and statistics." Statistics can be manipulated to prove the desired point, whatever it might be. For example, in a document entitled "Every Child Reading:

An Action Plan of the Learning First Alliance" and using NAEP statistics as well, a group of educators referring to themselves as the Learning First Alliance Board of Directors identify the continuing gap between White students and Black and Hispanic students. The group specifically cites that, "in 1994, 31 percent of white fourth graders scored below 'basic' [as readers on the NAEP],while 69 percent of African-American and 64 of Hispanic students did."

Be mindful that NAEP statistics were used to identify both progress and deficit for Black students. Which do we believe? I find the implied objectivity of test scores and statistics problematic for a variety of reasons. I am philosophically opposed to the notion that standardized tests actually measure student ability and intelligence or adequately predict future success.

Traditionally, scores on these tests have been used to support the intellectual inferiority claims made against Blacks, women, and second- and third-wave immigrants. Today, they are used to substantiate the same contentions, including those made in scabrous pieces of racial pornography such as Murray's and Herrnstein's *The Bell Curve* (1994) (that recycle ideas promulgated by Arthur Jensen approximately 30 years earlier) and similar ones used to support Proposition 209 and other such reactionary proposals that have arisen since its passage. Test scores merely obfuscate the issue.

Research seems to suggest that socioeconomic status is the greatest corollary to academic success. This message does not frequently reach the public. Instead, standardized tests are used to unfairly castigate poor children and those of color, as well as to provide a skewed rationale for the indictment of their parents and communities. Thus, the image remains intact that there is personal responsibility for poverty and that we, as a society, are exonerated from blame for it and relieved from the responsibility of helping to solve it.

Standardized testing has also proved problematic for a number of Black teachers who actually make it into the profession. With the widespread use of standardized teacher competency tests, the careers of many in this pool have ended prematurely or have been placed in serious jeopardy. The general consensus has been that many Black teachers and teachers from other historically disenfranchised racial and ethnic groups are unable to pass the test. Critics of the tests, however, state that they are "culturally bias[ed], lack . . . content and predictive validity, and . . . [are unable] to measure crucial effective qualities such as dedication, motivation, and caring," according to educational researcher

Jacqueline Jordan Irvine, in her book *Black Students and School Failure: Policies, Practices, and Prescriptions.*

But I am not Pollyanna-ish about the specter of standardized testing. I realize that as long as it remains a large industry, such testing will continue. I suggest, however, that this testing be considered only one measure in a number (like the use of portfolios and informal inventories) used to assess progress. The most significant concern before us is that students are receiving unequal educational opportunity, in spite of educational progress and gain (some of which have been documented in this chapter).

MISSED EDUCATIONAL OPPORTUNITIES

Crucial to the reader's understanding is an awareness that schools are sites of cultural and social reproduction. The same evils we face in society at large, we face within the school system. For instance, violence that plays itself out in schools is simply reflective of the violence that has been and remains a part of the world's cultural landscape.

Concomitantly, the racism, classism, and sexism that is the thread of American fabric is an integral dynamic of school culture as well, in terms of both the overt and hidden curriculums. The phrase *overt curriculum* refers to the curriculum that is explicitly taught to students through curriculum materials and instruction. The *hidden curriculum* refers to those messages about society, power, race, class, gender, and other positionalities that are transmitted subtly and implicitly to students through knowledge, attitudes, beliefs, rules, and practices.

In her chapter entitled "Knowledge Construction, Competing Critical Theories, and Education," scholar Beverly Gordon identifies Carter G. Woodson as possibly the first American educator to identify the way in which the education and schooling of American Blacks perpetuated the oppressive structures of racism and classism. He also suggested a culturally specific curriculum that highlighted the accomplishments of Blacks, focused on Black history, and geared education toward social action and racial uplift.

With these observations about the perpetuation of societal inequities highlighted, is it any wonder that we continue to have educational haves and have-nots? Even more alarming is that, quite frequently, the have-nots are children who are poor, of color, or both.

School districts servicing poor students, nationwide, often receive the lowest per-pupil expenditure rates and more than their fair share of inexperienced or unqualified teachers. Recent data support contentions that Black, Latino, and Native American children more frequently live in poverty. Students from these racial and ethnic groups are disproportionately placed in special education programs geared toward children with learning disabilities and emotional disturbances, yet they are underrepresented in classes for the gifted and talented. For example, Black students, especially males, are three times as likely to be placed in classes for the educable mentally retarded than White students, and one-half as likely to be placed in classes for the gifted and talented.

Children of color are frequently misdiagnosed with behavioral difficulties that require medication (such as Ritalin). In their book entitled *The War Against Children of Color: Psychiatry Targets Inner City Youth*, psychiatrist Peter Breggin and his wife Ginger have documented the way in which poor parents of color are being coerced into accepting Ritalin for their children by school systems nationwide. Special Education placements and pronouncements of alleged mental health disorders have long-lasting implications. They often remain with children for a lifetime and affect their chances for future success. For example, many children of color and the poor who are placed in special education ultimately become part of the criminal justice system. Similarly, children who are prescribed Ritalin are denied access to the military in later life. Although some parents might have serious reservations about military participation, the issue here is the limiting of options and choice.

Black and Latino boys are most frequently suspended, expelled from school, held over, and viewed by school authorities as deviant. In fact, one-third of all Black boys from low-income families are held over at least one grade. There is also a suggested correlation between being retained and dropping out of school.

As studies published during the Reagan-Bush era indicate, many of the students mentioned above (who left school prematurely) were categorized as failures (in respect to academic achievement and discipline) during the elementary school years.

Black girls have less interaction with their teachers than their White female counterparts, even though they initiate interaction much more frequently than White girls, White boys, and Black boys. They also receive less reinforcement than other children from their teachers.

Additionally, Black and Latino students are at greater risk than their White counterparts for teenage pregnancy, drug abuse, unemployment, underemployment, and involvement in the "prison industrial complex." I use the term "prison industrial complex," popularized by scholar and activist Angela Davis, because (as she has explained) it questions the very essence of a system in which the containment of Black and brown bodies has become an industry, an industry that supports the institution of capitalistic opportunism.

Race is only one aspect of this dilemma, however. Socioeconomic status compounds the difficulties faced by these children and young adults. That leaves parents (who have chosen to read this book) with one major question: What should I do to ensure my child's success in school generally and in literacy specifically?

ANSWERS

Most essentially, it is important that you begin early to provide your child with the foundations of educational success and literacy in your home before the child enters the school system. It is also important that parents and caregivers develop a partnership with the teachers and school systems servicing their children. After all, we are all supposed to be working toward the same goal: quality education and enhanced academic success for your child.

Parents, caregivers, and educators must establish a relationship that is based on mutual respect and the comprehensive understanding that we should all want what is best for our children. Further, it is important that these entities hold the others, as well as themselves, accountable. We must, collectively, demand the best for *all* children.

It is my sincere desire that this book serves as one step toward the development of true partnership between two groups that I hold dear.

Chapter 3

Comprehending Language and Culture

> One ever feels his two-ness, An American, a Negro; two souls, two thoughts, two unreconciled strivings; two warring ideals in one dark body, whose dogged strength alone keeps it torn asunder.
> —W.E.B. Du Bois, Philosopher and Scholar
> (*The Souls of Black Folk*)

Language is an entity that permeates every facet of our daily lives. It is symbolic, representative of thought and emotion. It provides us with a systematic way in which to convey messages; hence, it assists us in communication.

Language is in a perpetual state of flux. Standard American English, as constituted today, is not the same as that spoken during the 17th and 18th centuries. Words viewed as slang in the past two decades have been recently included in even the most noteworthy dictionaries. The American lexicon is continually expanding and redefining itself.

Language is transactional in nature. It aids us in the bartering of goods and services. It becomes essential that we use it proficiently to secure wants and needs. Our individual quests toward linguistic proficiency begin early and continue for a lifetime. Although language possesses many common traits, it also proves idiosyncratic.

LANGUAGE VARIATIONS

One of the most distinctive variations in language is known as the *dialect*. According to linguist J. L. Dillard (as noted in his book *Black*

English: Its History and Usage in the United States), a *dialect* is the collective linguistic patterns of a subgroup of the speakers of a language. If one employs this definition, Standard American English is merely a dialect of the English spoken in England.

Each dialect has grammar, characteristic pronunciation, verbal rituals, and vocabulary. Dialects are spoken around the world. They reflect geographic location, socioeconomic status, and other such factors. In many instances, dialects are accepted as different rather than deficit. Unfortunately, when oppression, race, or socioeconomic status intermingle with dialect, the dialects spoken by targeted groups are deemed substandard and inferior.

For instance, studies, expectedly, suggest that children who speak nonstandard English are disadvantaged in school. According to researchers Masahiko Minami and Carlos Ovando in a book chapter entitled "Language Issues in Multicultural Contexts"; "children from middle- and upper-class cultural and speech communities are sociolinguistically advantaged in the school environment, [while] children from poor, non-English and nonstandard English speech communities are more likely to be disadvantaged and even at risk of being marginalized in school environments" (p. 428).

Further, despite some of the historic information available on the acquisition of Black English Vernacular within the United States and presented in Chapter 1, the dialect continues to be viewed as subordinate. This view played front and center during the most recent Ebonics debate of 1996. The debate was sparked by educators in Oakland, California, proposing to use Ebonics in the classroom to move children toward standard English. The transition was designed to, ultimately, help Black children retain the beauty of their own dialect, yet understand the significance of effective and functional use of Standard American English.

Teaching Standard English as a Second Dialect is not a new phenomenon. Discussion concerning the necessity of different strategies to teach Black children Standard English can be traced back to the 18th century. The debate gained renewed verve during the 1960s and 70s and was reintroduced in 1996. But battles over language use in the classroom are not relegated solely to Blacks or the United States.

Within the confines of the United States, Latinos have long-fought struggles surrounding Bilingual Education and English as a Second Language. There has been disagreement regarding whether students should be totally immersed in English or placed in transitional classes that encourage the varied use of both their native languages and English. Controversy has also been fostered regarding the duration of Bilingual education and English as a Second Language placement.

Internationally, students have placed their lives in jeopardy, relative to the implications of classroom language use. For example, during the Soweto (South Africa) uprisings of 1976, students sacrificed themselves to protest the government-sanctioned imposition of Afrikaans (an official language of South Africa, developed from 17th-century Dutch) in the elementary school classroom.

To return to the 1996 Ebonics dilemma, however, there were flaws in Oakland's initial presentation of the idea. Yet, media distortion led the public to believe that children would be taught to speak Ebonics; a preposterous thought, considering that many youngsters enter the school building well-versed in the dialect. The illusory, media-driven perception of the debate brought out concerned Black political figures, activists, and pundits to denounce the plan; among them were Kwiesi Mfume, Maya Angelou, and Jesse Jackson (who, to his credit, later softened his criticism after understanding the concept more comprehensively). Noticeably absent from these televised debates, most times, were linguists, academics, and educators.

In many ways, mainstream fascination with this issue served to mask a greater problem. Why is it that an attempt to empower the historically disadvantaged is met with askance and indignation, when the maintenance of schools that fail urban center youngsters and burgeoning gaps in educational funding are not approached with such skepticism?

The Ebonics debate seemed to evoke pain for some sectors of the Black community. Some contended that the topic was painful because it revealed an aspect of Black life considered shameful. This argument does have a certain degree of merit. After all, Black English Vernacular has historically been used to denigrate the image of Blacks. For instance, many remember the Black slave or servant of the American cinema who served as the butt of jokes, providing White audiences with hearty laughs through the inadvertent use of *malapropisms* such as substitution of the word "pacific" for "specific" or "modiculous" rather than "ridiculous."

Within contemporary society, the appropriation of Black English Vernacular by Whites is viewed as cool, while use by Blacks remains, largely, unacceptable. Many of us recognize such appropriation and witness it today as White talk show hosts banter such phrases about as "you go, girl" and "we won't go there." Relatedly, whenever Black English Vernacular is criticized in the mainstream press, ethnic slang appears to be the focus. Yet, ethnic slang is only one aspect of Black English and predominantly used by Black youth, just as slang (generally) is most frequently used by teenagers (of all races and ethnicities) as a means of distinguishing themselves and maintaining group solidarity.

Black English Vernacular also has a proud heritage that must not be so easily relinquished. It is the speech of a displaced people who struggled to understand the language of their oppressors, as well as that of their fellow captives. Our ancestors adapted and developed a language of survival.

Black English Vernacular is part and parcel of the American lexicon and literary tradition. The hauntingly beautiful poetry and prose of Langston Hughes, Zora Neale Hurston, Amiri Baraka (LeRoi Jones), Haki Madhubuti (Don Lee), Nikki Giovanni, Alice Walker, and Toni Morrison attest to this truth.

Yet, the subject of Black English might also have proved painful because of the intense realization among Blacks that lack of facility with the language of power closes doors of access and limits upward mobility. It provides yet another way in which "to keep us down." The consistent use of Black English Vernacular is very closely tied to socioeconomic status. Most speakers of Black English Vernacular would be considered poor or working-class.

Traditionally, as Blacks (and other historically marginalized groups) have gained class mobility, the need for assimilation into the mainstream has also increased. As such, an aspect of that assimilation is the acceptance of Standard American English as "proper" or "correct" English.

Yet, Blacks of all classes, like all other racial and ethnic groups, *register-switch*. Register-switching refers to variation in speaking style. In other words, the way that one speaks with family and friends is not necessarily the way that one would speak in a work-related setting or formal meeting. Similarly, there may be phrases used in one's town, city, or province that would only be understood by other members of that community. One would probably use a different manner of explanation for a person who was not from the community (if understanding was desired).

It is equally important to state that there are individual differences in respect to the dialect spoken by any group. These differences that are unique for each person are referred to as *idiolects*.

As can be ascertained from this discussion regarding the impact of race, ethnicity, socioeconomic status, geographic region, and age on dialect, language is closely related to culture.

LANGUAGE AS AN ASPECT OF CULTURE

Through the vehicle of language, distinct cultural information is acquired. Culture is defined as "the knowledge, ideas and skills that enable a group to survive," according to anthropologist Brian Bullivant (as quoted in *Multicultural Education: Issues and Perspectives,* 2nd Edition by James Banks and Cherry A. McGee Banks). Language helps us to express that knowledge, idea, and skill.

Since the focus of this book is Blacks within the United States and the group meets the definition of culture provided, it will be referred to as such. It is the contention of this author that U.S. Black culture is distinctive from other racial and ethnic cultures. A caveat must be provided for this statement, however. By distinguishing U.S. Black culture, I do not wish to speak about it in an essentialist or binary manner. One cannot speak emphatically, stating that all Blacks as a group or culture do one thing or the other. There are variations within cultural groups.

One can be a member of different cultures simultaneously; such membership is not mutually exclusive. Cultures can be formed on the basis of gender, socioeconomic status, religion, disability, and sexual orientation, as well as race and ethnicity. Varying cultural membership can also create conflict. For instance, Black women and men sometimes conflict on the issue of gender, in spite of the fact that they share race. Class-based differences also prompt the creation of cultural divides among Blacks. In other instances, Blacks who migrate to this country voluntarily are sometimes at odds with Blacks whose history reflects involuntary immigration status.

Neither do I claim that distinguishing features shared by U.S. Blacks make them superior or inferior to other racial or ethnic groups. I do not wish to attempt the reproduction of an ideology of oppression that has been exceedingly cruel to my own people. I simply maintain that there are certain aspects of culture that U.S. Blacks share and that shared culture makes them different from other such groups.

For example, we share the legacy of slavery and the devastation that that institution wreaked on our social, political, and economic networks. We share the pain and acknowledgment of racism, discrimination, and prejudice. We also share a resiliency that has enabled us to survive in a frequently hostile and schizophrenic society that devalues and denigrates Black life. Many of us have learned adaptive mechanisms that enable us to cope in such an environment, in optimal fashion, ensuring both individual and group survival.

Culture is also transmitted from one generation to the next. Elders help to enculturate the youngest group members by providing them with a sense of group values and identity. The youngest members of our cultural group learn what it means to be Black in the United States from us, their parents, caregivers, and adult role models.

THE ROLE OF PARENTS AND CAREGIVERS

In today's society, the role of parent or caregiver is an increasingly challenging one. I often share with my mother and sister that it is easier for me to teach approximately 45 students, confer with them on upcoming projects, plan curriculum, grade papers, and attend meetings in a day than it is to remain at home, caring for my two-year-old daughter and infant son. Although the job of a parent or caregiver is infinitely rewarding, it is difficult as well.

The hope of all parents and caregivers is to provide their children with the best that life has to offer. The determination of success, however, is totally reliant on outcome (how does one's child turn out). Within the social sciences, the efficacy of parents has, traditionally, been determined by applying a Eurocentric standard and creating false dichotomies. One was identified as either a good parent or a bad one, as determined by these standards. But such an analysis is far too simplistic to explain a phenomenon as complex and intricate as parenting.

As discussed in Holden's *Parents and the Dynamics of Child Rearing*, John Ogbu suggests that the issue of cultural relativity greatly affects parenting. For instance, Euro-American parents in suburban environments might value creativity and critical thinking in children. They might encourage their children to question and challenge authority. They are not conditioned to believe that such behavior could have deadly consequences. Their worldview and experiences would be incongruent with such a belief, in most instances.

Conversely, many Black parents (of all stations in life) might value obedience more than creativity, for they realize that any diversion from that path could prove life-threatening. During the era of Jim Crow, questioning authority could result in lynching or violence, especially for male children. Today, it can result in death at the hands of police or those of one's own people.

Whereas some parents are better prepared to actively pursue the goal of influential parenting because of effective models, support networks, and strong desire, others need a little more assistance and reassurance.

Sometimes parents who are involved with drugs, in prison, or other at-risk situations feel that they have nothing positive to add to their children's lives. There is the sense that everything in which they are involved turns out poorly; a sense of hopelessness pervades. As a result, it is occasionally easier for these parents to, emotionally as well as physically, relinquish their responsibility to other caregivers. I would say to this group of parents that, in spite of challenges, they can still positively impact their children's lives. The desire to be an effective parent means a great deal. The fact that you are reading this book reflects your concern for your child's well-being.

Although the role of parent or caregiver is hard generally, its difficulty is compounded for parents with children of color. The parents and caregivers of such children are their children's first tutors in learning self-respect; forming a positive, race-conscious identity; understanding their histories; and navigating in an environment that is infrequently kind. In their book *Raising Black Children*, psychiatrists James Comer and Alvin Poussaint state that parents should "model and teach their children that they are not just Black, and certainly not just American, but both simultaneously."

Chapter 4

Infants, Toddlers, and Emergent Literacy

My mother read poetry to me before I could read, and I can't remember when I couldn't read. We grew up with books. I don't think you can write if you don't read. You can't read if you can't think. Thinking, reading and writing all go together. When I was about eight, I decided that the most wonderful thing, next to a human being, was a book.

—Margaret Walker, Novelist (as quoted in Tamara Nikuradse's *My Mother Had a Dream: African-American Women Share Their Mothers' Words of Wisdom*)

As a result of their interactions with us, children learn the dialect or language that we speak and that of the communities in which we live. Children learn language through their interactions with other social beings and the environment. Although some lessons are conveyed verbally, many are taught by example.

Most children are able to miraculously comprehend complex grammatical systems and acquire remarkable vocabularies without any formal instruction. By the time most children reach the age of three, they can use approximately 1,000 words and a variety of sentences to express themselves. This figure of 1,000 includes those words in the child's expressive language repertoire (the child's ability to say words). The child's receptive repertoire (understanding what is said) might include 2,000 to 3,000 additional words, according to early literacy researcher

Dr. Lesley Mandel Morrow in her book *Literacy Development in the Early Years: Helping Children Read and Write.*

Emergent literacy, a term that evolved during the early 1980s, focuses on a child's earliest efforts toward literacy development. In reiteration, *literacy*, as defined by multicultural literacy expert Kathryn Au, in her book *Literacy Instruction in Multicultural Settings*, involves "the ability and willingness to use reading and writing to construct meaning from printed text." The process of emergent literacy begins at birth and continues until the child is able to use language and literacy effectively, for her or his own purposes.

LANGUAGE ACQUISITION

There are some things known about language development that are applicable to *all* children. Most emergent literacy experts contend that the language acquisition process begins at birth; yet, there are a growing number of us who believe that it actually begins earlier, in utero (in the womb).

From the time that children are first held in the arms of parents or caregivers, they are immersed in language. After all, we speak to newborns. We call their names, tell them ours, and provide them with appellations for objects surrounding them. We serve as language role models for them. "A parent is a child's first mentor on what words mean and how to mean things with words. A parent is a child's first tutor in unraveling the fascinating puzzle of written language" states the seminal *Becoming A Nation of Readers: The Report of the Commission on Reading.*

From the beginning, infants demonstrate that they have been affected by our efforts to communicate with them. They coo, babble, and move their tiny bodies in the direction of voices and sounds heard. They are able to immediately recognize some of those sounds, especially the voice of their mothers. Some of these simple and minute acts, that may be taken for granted, become representative of children's first attempts to understand language and use it to interact with others.

INFANTS AND LANGUAGE DEVELOPMENT

Because children begin so early in their attempts to make sense of language, it is perfectly appropriate to begin actively working on your child's literacy development during infancy. Initial efforts should involve the development of language skills. As per the dictates of this discussion, a distinction will be made between infants and toddlers by classifying infants as 0 to 18 months and toddlers as 18 months to 3 years.

The first step in influencing your infant's language development involves surrounding him or her with talk. As you tend to your child's daily needs (bathing, feeding, diapering, and pampering), explain that you are changing diapers, feeding, or otherwise engaging in the process of making her more comfortable.

Reassure your baby of your return whenever you leave him (whether the leave has been precipitated by the need or desire to return to work or simply run an errand). On returning, tell the infant that he was missed. Although this point might prove pedantic for some, its necessity will be addressed in upcoming paragraphs.

The growing number of women working outside the home has prompted much debate about the potentially harmful effects that working mothers have on their children. On its face, this argument appears sexist. It seems to release fathers from their responsibility or diminish their roles in the rearing of children.

Within the context of a society in which the mainstream finds it necessary for both parents to work, working outside the home is often an economic reality for people of color and the poor. Many classified as poor are single mothers who work every day as opposed to receiving governmental support. This point about the poor is emphasized, in an attempt to counter claims that vilify women of color as "welfare queens." These claims are routinely made in the media, when reality disproves the claim. The majority of welfare recipients remains White and female. As it currently stands, however, Whites appear to get off welfare rolls faster than their Black counterparts.

For many people of color, the effect of work on their children can best be described as a nonissue, especially when it provides food, shelter, and clothing for the children in their charge. So, rather than spending time feeling guilty about leaving your child, make the best of the experience. You are teaching a valuable lesson about trust, dependability, and love by telling your child that you will return when you leave the home and making good on that promise.

Tell infants on a continuing basis that you love them, appreciate them, and that your life has been changed for the better by their mere presence.

It seems that we (as a people) sometimes have difficulty with this expression. I grew up in a household in which my mother told us, "Love is an action." The translation was, "I feed you, clothe you, and keep a roof over your head. That is proof that I love you." Although I know intuitively that she loves me, the expression of that love was primarily tacit. It has been my experience, through dialogue, that many other Blacks grew up in this fashion. As a result, I would caution that while it is important to *show* your children that you love them, it is equally important to *tell* them.

Respond to your infant's attempts to communicate with you. Act as if you are engaged in conversation with him. Lastly, model effective speech; make certain that you pronounce words distinctly. Remember, tiny and unfamiliar ears are attempting to grasp the words that you use.

Many of the suggestions provided in this subsection have been quite general. To a certain extent, I hold the view that the *best* education for all children is also the *best* for Black children; thus the *best* information for all parents is also the *best* information for Black parents. But there are facets of this discussion, on language and literacy development in infants, that are most pertinent to the parents of Black children. For example, it has already been established that we live in a society that demonstrates its hostility toward Black life on an ongoing basis. The fight to sustain one's self, in spite of this perpetual barrage, begins at birth and continues for a lifetime.

The first step in this struggle is to learn to love one's self. It is the parent or caregiver's responsibility to initiate this process and teach Black children to love themselves. Talk assists us in this venture. Learn to affirm your infant's racial identity through complimenting her on racial features. Positively reinforce pride in such features. For example, as you bathe your baby, comment on her "beautiful chocolate-colored skin, pretty dark eyes, and magnificent curly hair." Talk to the baby about your racial features and those of your partner or spouse. These compliments are quite significant because your child will, ultimately, be able to detect your feelings about race from the words you speak.

Surround your infant with positive and realistic images of Blackness via photographs, art work, and, most important, *books*. Some of the books chosen should validate your child's emerging racial self-concept through illustrations. These representations should realistically highlight the physical beauty and diversity of Blacks, in addition to providing healthy portraits of Black life.

At this point, some readers might be wondering whether I am suggesting that books be read to infants. A few might even be wondering if such a practice is merely an exercise in futility.

Let me preface my responses by saying that I understand the skepticism. I had a similar reaction when a preservice teacher (in one of my evening classes) told me that she taught infants to read during the day. After a chuckle, I asked, "How?" She smiled, then responded, "The first lesson is don't eat the book." I smiled, acknowledging that it was an appropriate place to start.

INFANTS AND READING ALOUD

In response to your concerns, I *am* suggesting that reading to infants is purposeful rather than futile. "The single most important activity for building eventual success in reading is reading aloud to children," states *Becoming a Nation of Readers*. Once again, it is best to start early.

But what are the benefits of reading aloud to infants? As my student suggested, the first benefit involves the simple concept of book handling. As a result of being read to, infants learn that books are held gently and pages are turned. Books for infants come in a variety of sturdy and durable materials, such as heavy cardboard, cloth, and plastic, for the express purpose of being handled.

Second, reading aloud to infants provides them with positive, affective experiences with books. The internal motivation to read does impact reading proficiency. Most people who desire to read (of their own volition rather than as directed by external forces) have had positive experiences with it. A component of reading ability centers on the *affective*, the emotions attached.

Some of my earliest and fondest recollections include my grandparents reading picture storybooks to me that my mother had sent. Then, the books served as the lifeline between my mother and me as we were temporarily separated. I vividly remember sitting on my grandmother's lap (or my mother's when she visited) and being read to. I can still feel the skin of the reader against my own and the smell of the reader's perfume and warm breath. These experiences with *lap reading* proved powerful enough to instill a lifelong love of reading in me. I believe that, with early exposure, it can have this effect on any reader.

Finally, through reading aloud, infants are receiving yet another opportunity during which to be exposed to language. They hear words and the way they are pronounced. Yet, unlike the other benefits, this one might be achieved through the use of audiotapes featuring songs, lullabies, and nursery rhymes as well.

As you talk to infants about the book you are reading, they also learn that talk and good books accommodate each other.

TODDLERS AND TALK

Toddlers, classified as 18 months to 3 years, have distinct personalities, more words at their command, and are more adept than infants are at communicating their needs and desires. It becomes quite apparent that toddlers have agendas of their own.

Most toddlers have spoken their first words prior to this point of development. They are now using two forms of speech proficiently. *Holophrastic speech* (in which one word is used to express complex ideas) emerges. For instance, your toddler might say "cooks" and point at the cookie box to express the more complex thought, "I want cookies." Holophrastic speech develops into *telegraphic speech* once the child has an adequate grasp of word order in sentences. Telegraphic speech occurs when the child uses more than one word to communicate thought but not an entire sentence. For example, "see car" becomes representative of "I see the car."

The need for talk between parent or caregiver and child increases for toddlers. It is essential that the talk initiated during infancy continue. It is also important to increase verbal demands on your child and yourself. Now that the toddler has a more comprehensive understanding of words and their utility, require that he use them to communicate.

As your child points at a thing desired, encourage him to ask for the object prior to fulfilling the wish. Further, as you are in the process of wish-fulfillment, model (in sentence form) the child's request. For example, if he points to a bottle of milk and says "ba-ba," give him milk. Simultaneously say, "You want your bottle now. Let me get it for you."

Also, for the purpose of encouraging language growth, introduce the concept of language accuracy. As you teach your child the names of body parts, use anatomically correct terminology. Such accuracy is especially significant in relation to the genitals. By referring to your child's genitals as "vagina" or "penis" and encouraging the child to do so, you are modeling accuracy and concomitantly sending the message that there is nothing shameful about them. As we attempt to mask genitals with pet names, we display our level of discomfort with those areas. After all, we do not frequently invent pet names to describe arms, legs, and hands.

In discussing verbal expectations of toddlers, it becomes essential to broach the subjects of courteous communication and good manners. In this author's opinion, an ever-increasing lack of kindness and compassion has reached epidemic proportions within American culture. This epidemic is merely symptomatic of a larger problem: lack of respect. Such disrespect can be witnessed as some of our youth respond to a society, which regularly communicates its sense that they are expendable, by placing more value in "*mobile status symbols*" (a term popularized by Marilyn Kern-Foxworth) such as athletic shoes and designer clothing than the youth place on each other's lives.

Unfortunately, disrespect is also communicated from parent or caregiver to child by excessive use of *command talk*, such as "sit down now" or "be quiet." Some parents use command talk much more regularly than others. As a result, their children's speech and ability to communicate remain underdeveloped for the most part.

It is my contention that the use of this form of communication is unintentional. After all, most parents want the best for their children and would never intentionally do anything that would cause harm. Some parents, however, use command talk as a means of reinforcing the need for obedience in children. Others are simply parenting in the same fashion in which they were parented. Possibly, reflection on the latter reason is needed. Was the way in which you were parented without flaw or could it benefit from improvement?

Another sector of parents are aligned in their belief that explanation is excessively time-consuming. Yet, if you do not have the time for your children now, when will you have the time? Time invested in your children now can save on time spent dealing with their problems during adulthood.

Relatedly, command talk can connote ownership of children. I once heard a saying that has remained with me until this day. It, basically, states that children do not belong to us, they are merely on loan from God. Thus, it is our responsibility to serve as guides and lead by example rather than force and compulsion.

Children are reliant on us to teach values, especially those of kindness and compassion. We teach these simple lessons through simple modes, such as the way in which we speak to our children and others. Speak kindly to your children in as many instances as possible and require that they speak kindly as well. Emphasize the use of "please" and "thank you." Show empathy when your children expresses sadness or anger. Teach them to talk about feelings and think about them before acting.

Finally, talk and a wide range of experience greatly affect a child's eventual capacity to read. You can provide your child with the needed experience by taking him on trips and discussing those trips. In homes in which there is more than one child, it is important to take children on outings as a group and as individuals, thus, conveying the significance of the family unit, as well as each member of the unit.

Trips can be basic and/or exotic, as dictated by your financial situation or time constraints. Don't underestimate the value of trips to the library, the supermarket, the park, the beach, the zoo, and local cultural events.

For instance, many libraries have story times for toddlers and special events, such as magic shows, musical programs, and puppet shows. It is also good to initiate toddlers into the world of reading by helping them to get a library card and borrowing books from the library.

However, for those who are able to provide such experiences, toddlers can also benefit from trips that expose them to national sites, as well as those considered global in scope.

TODDLERS AND TELEVISION

Surrounding toddlers with language might involve television for some parents. Quite candidly, television is often vilified. Many talk about the content of television shows without discussing parental responsibility as it pertains to children's viewing. Parents should be critical consumers of television and encourage the development of their children in similar fashion.

For this author, watching television is not inherently harmful. It is a tool that can be used for purposes of entertainment, education, and the widespread proliferation of political messages and agendas. When television assumes the role of baby-sitter or its messages are accepted as truth, it becomes harmful. Television should be enjoyed in short, commercial-free time spans (30 minutes to an hour a sitting) by toddlers. The segments should be commercial-free because your child should benefit from television programming without being sucked into the massive consumerism that it encourages. You, as parent or caregiver, would like to determine the toys and foods deemed appropriate for your child as opposed to having such decisions made for you with the help of slick marketing campaigns. Remember, television is designed to turn a profit. It is an industry.

There are a number of quality, commercial-free children's programs, such as *Sesame Street, Reading Rainbow, Gullah Gullah Island*, and *Arthur*, that can provide your child with worthwhile information and skills. These programs have a specific focus on literacy that I find admirable.

Yet, criticisms of these programs are also existent. For example, criticism of *Sesame Street* seems to abound, especially as large scale, conservative efforts have been made to eliminate it in recent years. Many conservative critics view the show as another aspect of public television broadcasting that should not necessitate support from the common taxpayer. It is considered a frill by this constituency. Some educators and psychologists contend that the show lacks educational value because of its flashy presentation, bright lights, and colors.

Sesame Street, which first aired on November 10, 1969, was designed as a component of children's television that would "give great attention to the informal educational needs of preschool children, particularly to interest and help children whose intellectual and cultural preparation might otherwise be less than adequate," according to a report submitted by The Carnegie Commission on Educational Television. Although some might find aspects of the report's wording questionable, it was a liberal effort toward "social reform."

As a critical viewer, I have noted *Sesame Street*'s emphasis on multiculturalism; ability to engage young viewers in a fashion unparalleled by other such programs; attempts to advocate gender and race equity; and subtle teaching of values such as love, sharing, and cooperation. Concomitantly, there is reinforcement of basic educational concepts.

For me, there is educational children's programming that I find reprehensible. There is the insidious presence of the Disney production that many parents should find alarming. Disney is a huge, profit-turning conglomerate. As such, it wields powerful economic and political force. In spite of its sponsorship of programs celebrating education, scholarships, and financial aid to underprivileged youngsters, Disney movies have been frequently cited for their racist portrayals. We can look back to the defiled images of people of color in both *Song of the South* (1946) and *The Jungle Book* (1967). The use of dark coloring in the animated presentation of villains, in contrast to the ethereal coloring and "whiteness" of the good can be scrutinized.

More recently, we can examine the racialized voices of the hyenas in *The Lion King* (1994), the nefarious portrayal of Arabs in *Aladdin* (1989), and the emphasis on cross-cultural understanding and love that masks the genocide and rampant colonization of Native Americans in *Pocahontas* (1995).

Further, I believe that it is incumbent on Black consumers of Disney products to reflect on their consumption, in the spirit of unity among people of the African Diaspora. Maybe consideration should be given to the widely distributed and televised reports that Disney, in recent years, paid Haitian workers 25 cents per hour for the production of T-shirts and other paraphernalia sold in its stores. Quite clearly, profit was made on the backs of Blacks and Disney was complicitous in their exploitation.

These points lead us back to a continuing theme in this book, the development of racial self-concept.

TODDLERS AND RACIAL DEVELOPMENT

There is documentation that infants as young as six months of age notice skin color differentiations. By age two to three, children readily question skin color and learn to attach value to such difference. As an example, a friend's daughter asked her if God loved White people. My friend responded, "Yes, God loves all of us." But she was left reflecting on the question and its motivation. As she thought, she came to the realization that her child attended a predominantly Black and Latino school, had few opportunities to interact with people of other races, and the only books she purchased featured Black people. Resultantly, her child had come to question whether God loved Whites.

After that encounter, my friend committed herself to providing greater opportunity for her daughter to experience cross-cultural exchange and read more books that featured characters from varying racial and ethnic groups.

Although the example provided centers on a Black child, Euro-American children also receive messages about race as a result of their environments and responses to their questions. For example, it seems evident that many White children learn early in life that whiteness is the "norm" or the "average." They might be taught that racialized difference is impolite to notice or comment on. Such messages can be reinforced by parents who respond to questions about race with embarrassment or harsh words. They can also be transmitted through cultural artifacts and media images (such as advertisements, sports, magazines, books, and movies) that glorify whiteness and hold Nordic racial features as the standard of beauty.

All parents need to broach the subject of racialized difference in a positive fashion. Through this means, children will come to understand that there should be acceptance of people across lines of race and ethnicity.

The use of books for this purpose is highly commendable. Although Black parents should continue to reinforce the beauty and diversity of Black life through books that they introduced during their children's infancy, they should also begin to broaden their children's views of the world and humanity. Books should help children to value their own qualities through both comparison and contrast.

At this point, some parents might wonder if there is a contradiction in my message. Am I now displaying selective amnesia, forgetting about the racism and discrimination we (as a people) have faced? Absolutely not! But I think that clarification should be provided on the way in which I use the word "racism." In his book *Portraits of White Racism*, author David Wellman defines racism as a "system of advantage based upon race." Thus the advantage created by whiteness can afford those with white skin opportunity and access that people of color don't share. Whites benefit (whether in acknowledged or unacknowledged fashion) from both white skin privilege and racism.

Yet, according to psychologist Beverly Daniel Tatum (in her book *Why Are All The Black Kids Sitting Together in the Cafeteria?: And Other Conversations About Race*), all people potentially hold racial prejudices and sometimes those prejudices lead individuals to commit "hateful acts." I feel that it proves important for parents and caregivers of Black children to introduce and reinforce the facts that institutions, such as racism, can disadvantage us and people can display racist, prejudiced, or hateful behavior; but there are good people in each race and ethnicity.

BOOKS AND TODDLERS

Reading books to toddlers is somewhat different from reading to infants. In some ways, it is amazing to note the difference that a few short months make. Toddlers are more apt in both attention span and comprehension level. Make certain that you provide opportunities to read aloud each day. Some parents, however, might choose to read to their children several times a day. Make reading aloud a celebratory act.

You should continue lap reading, but also attempt to make reading aloud a ritual in your home. Possibly, your child will enjoy reading just before bedtime as a means of winding down. Some parents might choose to read stories during meals, and others still might choose to read at bath time. You will choose, accordingly, as per the demands of your own schedule. Set time aside for reading without interference from the television. This simple practice helps to cement the belief that reading is special in your child's mind.

Take books for your child to enjoy as the family goes on outings (e.g., the doctor's office, to run errands, and extended car trips).

Also related to the celebration of books, parents and caregivers should give their children books as gifts or gift certificates to bookstores. Encourage family friends and relatives to follow suit. Some might feel that books are not fun gifts, but keep in mind that children adopt their attitudes about reading from us. Not only does the practice of giving books as gifts encourage reading, it quite directly sends a message about the value you place on education and literacy in general.

As you read to toddlers, encourage both their comments and questions. Stop at intervals and ask them whether they like the story, what they think about the illustrations, the characters, and their actions. Also, identify the parts of the book for them. Call attention to the title and the author's name.

At this point, I feel the need to address one group of parents quite specifically, single parents. Sometimes, fatigue seems to fight for your child's reading time. As a result of my own experience, I am knowledgeable of the struggle for time and resources that single parents face. I would ask that you battle fatigue and take a few minutes to read to your child, at least once per day. You will reap the rewards as your child develops proficiency in reading and comes to value education and literacy because of the example that you have set.

During times when you simply can not read, ask another family member to do so for the purposes of establishing continuity and reinforcing that the activity is important. We have already determined that *families* play the most influential roles in the development of early and proficient readers.

Chapter 5

The Preschool Reader and Writer

My mother was not one to offer words of wisdom. Instead, she led by example. She was curious about everything—the mundane to the profound. For her, all experiences were learning opportunities. My mother often read what I was reading, from Dr. Seuss to Friedrich Nietzsche. Then, we would have full-blown debates about ideas. She would often thank me for teaching her something new. In short, my mother always took me seriously. She simply assumed that I would be successful in whatever I did.
—Linda A. Hill, First African American woman
to receive tenure at the Harvard Business School (as
quoted in Tamara Nikuradse's *My Mother Had a Dream:
African-American Women Share Their
Mothers' Words of Wisdom*)

The language capabilities of preschoolers (identified here as three- and four-year-olds) develop at breakneck speed. Their vocabularies expand. Their knowledge of sentence structure and levels of comprehension grow. They use language more proficiently than they did as toddlers. In many ways, their speech resembles adult speech.

ORAL LANGUAGE DEVELOPMENT

Talk *remains* essential for them. It also becomes quite exciting for both children and parents or caregivers. At this age, children begin to master a more efficient and effective mode of communication. They can meet their needs of self-expression through talk. For parents, it is a joy to realize that your child can now converse with you.

It becomes increasingly important to talk and listen to your children on a frequent basis. Talk with them about things that prove meaningful to them. Ask questions about activities in which they are involved, as well as those regarding their likes, dislikes, feelings, hopes, fears, and dreams.

Ask questions that are *open-ended*; questions that require more than a yes or no answer or a specific bit of information. Open-ended questions give children an opportunity to think about their responses and use their creativity. Ask *genuine* questions during conversation, those to which you truly seek an answer. Also, provide children appropriate time to think about the questions they have been asked and respond.

As you converse, sit close to your child and clearly convey the sense that you are listening. Talk without interruption from the television or radio and set aside special times during which to talk. For some, this time might be dinnertime or the child's bathtime. For others, it might be the time during which the family is preparing for or en route to work or school.

Another oral language development strategy that children usually enjoy is storytelling and the sharing of personal experience. Tell your child about your life as a child. What things did you enjoy? What were your favorite pastimes and experiences?

Children also like hearing details that intertwine your life with theirs. For instance, how did you meet your child's other parent or caregiver? Are there circumstances surrounding his birth that you are willing to share at this point? What does "family" mean to you? What are your hopes and dreams for your family? You will find that, with time, your child will be able to tell *your* stories from memory and eagerly anticipate other such tales that you have to offer.

Singing songs and reciting nursery rhymes also help both toddlers and preschoolers develop language capabilities.

PRESCHOOLERS AND PRINT AWARENESS

As with talk, many of the language and literacy practices initiated during your child's infancy and toddlerhood should continue during the preschool years. The only significant change in these practices is that they gradually become more sophisticated.

For example, in developing your infant's print awareness, the concepts broached were simple. For the most part, they focused on book-handling and affective qualities associated with language and literacy. As a preschooler, however, your child's print repertoire should broaden and expand. Reading researcher Ken Goodman describes four types of encounters with print that your child should have in the home prior to entering school. The encounters include those with environmental print, informational reading, occupational reading and reading for leisure.

Environmental print is print seen within the physical environment. Environmental print includes logos such as those used by McDonald's and Burger King, those that children easily recognize on boxes of their favorite breakfast cereals and toothpastes, as well as street signs. Many children, as young as two years old, readily recognize restaurant logos.

Parents or caregivers can assist in the development of their children's recognition of such print by helping with identification. As you cross the street, point out street signs that direct us to walk or caution us to wait. Before entering a public restroom with your daughter or son, ask which sign is representative of her or his gender. While driving, ask children to aid you by identifying specific signs, landmarks, and logos. Also, ask them to help in the grocery store and around the house while simultaneously providing them with opportunities to use environmental print. For instance, as you stand close by, ask your child to get the toothpaste you regularly use or juice she drinks and place it in the shopping cart. Use each such moment as a teachable one.

Informational reading includes reading done for the purpose of obtaining information. There should be opportunities for your child to see you initiate the process of information-gathering through the use of books, magazines, and newspapers. For instance, if you and your child are going to bake a cake, first select an appropriate recipe to follow from a cookbook or magazine.

If planning to see a movie, peruse the newspaper with your child in an effort to determine what is playing, start times, and locations. Even a disadvantageous situation, such as getting lost, might prove productive if you use the opportunity to find your way with a map.

In these ways, children not only make the connection between information-seeking and reading, they also learn that reference materials are used differently from pleasure books.

Occupational reading conveys essential information about both reading and attitudes about work or employment. Children's attitudes about work or employment develop as a result of their interactions with parents and caregivers. If our words and actions convey the sense that work (domestic or professional) is pleasurable and valued, children perceive work as such. Conversely, if work or employment is despised and disrespected, children begin to associate work with displeasure.

At this point, some readers might ask, "What if I really do hate my job? Isn't it dishonest to pretend otherwise?" These questions could be answered in a number of ways. I will focus on two. First, you might hate your job, but I doubt that you hate the financial freedom it plausibly brings. Thus, work is not pleasurable for you, but it is necessary and valued. The second response involves the fact that your dislike of your job might prompt you to seek another that more appropriately satisfies your needs. In this way, you are also teaching your child valuable lessons about job satisfaction and taking an active role in creating change.

In an effort to show that work is important and valued, parents and caregivers should provide their children with opportunities to see them reading about their work. Whether you are a mechanic, cashier, homemaker, teacher, or physician, there should be some work-related or professional material that can be read and shared with your child. I am not necessarily suggesting that very young children will understand the jargon used and concepts presented. But caregivers can always explain or summarize the reading for them. Most important, children will understand that you consider your work meaningful.

The value of *reading for leisure* can prove difficult for parents to impress on their youngsters, especially if its love has not been fostered early. Frequently, I encounter parents who complain that their older children rarely pick up a book to read for leisure. I have also encountered a number of new college admits and sophomores who proudly boast that they have never read a book all the way through that was not assigned.

Although I understand that books increasingly compete with other forms of media (e.g., television, the Internet, CD players), friends, and sleep, I am also aware that, for many young people and their parents and caregivers, reading is not a priority in their homes. If a parent or caregiver desires that her or his child read for pleasure, the best possible insurance is to serve as a role model and start early.

Allow your children to see you reading books and periodicals that interest you. Have your children accompany you to the library on a rainy day rather than to the video store. Talk to them about your reading and share excerpts. Finally, plan and implement family reading events during which televisions, radios, and computers are shut off and you all read for an allotted period of time. In respect to duration, it would probably be best to start off in small increments of time (e.g., 15 minutes) and work your way up. Hold book discussion groups with family members that focus on a shared reading or interest.

Many of Goodman's encounters with print seem to primarily focus on your position as a literacy role model. Yet, it remains significant to continue providing your preschool child with the encounters with books that you initiated during her infancy and toddlerhood, enhancing them as well.

EXPERIENCES WITH BOOK PRINT IN THE HOME

Reading books to your son should now be a routine practice. The array of print materials to which your child is exposed should expand to include newspapers and magazines. If possible, invest in a children's magazine subscription.

These suggestions are not meant to be financially daunting, however. You can find books that are moderately priced ($3.95 to $6.95) at local bookstores. Frequently, the problem with large chain bookstores is not the price of the books; rather, it is the lack of available children's or adolescent books featuring racially diverse characters. If you find that this problem exists at your local bookstore, get together with other Black parents or a racially diverse group and collectively demand that bookstores stock more of such books. Corporations speak the language of profit and understand potential purchasing power or lack thereof best.

If your budget does not permit the routine purchase of books, remember library use is free and newspapers can be purchased at nominal cost.

In respect to book selection, preschool children tend to like books that contain rhymes and stories with predictable patterns, as well as concept books, such as the alphabet, counting or shapes. You might find that four-year-olds have slightly more sophisticated literary tastes, preferring longer and more complex stories, such as simple folk tales and fairy tales. But permit me a word of caution about traditional fairy tales.

Many American parents, of all races, grew up with traditional fairy tales such as *Cinderella* and *Snow White*. Although feminist critics, such as Andrea Dworkin, have successfully identified flaws in these tales regarding the portrayal of women as either passive and desiring rescue by a man or potent, ugly, and evil, there are racial implications attached to such tales as well.

What messages are sent to children of color when they are bombarded with Eurocentric, blonde, and blue-eyed concepts of beauty? What do they learn about their own complexions, hair, and physical features? Additionally, what do they learn about villains? Is it possible they learn that, in many instances, villains resemble them? After all, villains have been traditionally featured as dark in hue or wearing dark clothing.

Another group of people commonly stereotyped as villains include the disabled. Why is Rumpelstilskin or Captain Hook a villain? Why does it take seven dwarfs to compose one human personality? It seems, to this reader at least, that the answer lies solely in their disabilities.

Parents and caregivers should also consider who privileges certain tales. For instance, the European (French and German) versions of *Cinderella* were not the first documented. History suggests that the oldest variant of *Cinderella* is the Chinese *Yeh Shen*. It also appears as if the Native American variants, *The Rough-Faced Girl* and *Sootface*, predated *Cinderella* as most Americans know it.

Am I suggesting that you refrain from exposing your children to fairy tales? No. Instead I am suggesting that you use them selectively and expose your children to fairy tales from around the world. I also believe that these books can be used as sites for critical inquiry with your child. You might choose to ask pivotal questions about beauty standards (for example, what makes a person beautiful?) and the portrayal of certain groups of people. I am sure that a provocative discussion should result.

As your preschooler grows, your purposes for reading with her will change. During infancy, you read so that your child would see realistic images of self and acquire simple book concepts. Once your child was a toddler, you read to establish reading as an aspect of daily life in your home.

Now that your preschooler is three or four years of age, your purposes become even more sophisticated. Your child is now able to understand *conventions of book print*. As you read to your child presently, he is able to recognize (with your direction) that books contain letters, words (that move from left to right), sentences, and punctuation.

The child may also distinguish between pleasure books and informational texts. The preschooler will eventually understand that pleasure stories are read from front to back, feature illustrations, and possess a beginning, middle, and end in addition to having plots, characters, settings, and so forth, whereas using information books, conversely, we turn to the specific pages that are needed.

In order to ensure that your child grasps such necessary conventions of pleasure books, per se, identify the title and author of books before reading them. Point to illustrations and ask the child to tell the story by its pictures before reading. Follow the text with your finger so that the direction in which book print goes is easily detected. Pause periodically and encourage your child to ask questions about the reading. After completing the reading selection, talk to your child about the book read or ask her or him to retell it.

You do not necessarily have to use all of these strategies during one reading. Do not make your reading sessions so routine that they become boring for your child. Vary the strategies; have your child retell the story during one sitting, and focus on telling the story through the illustrations during another. Through using these simple techniques, you are attempting to strengthen your child's reading *comprehension* (understanding what is being read).

HOME EXPERIENCES WITH WRITING

All children have the potential to develop naturally as writers, just as they can become speakers and readers. Generally, children experience stages of development in relation to writing and spelling. Although all children seem to experience these stages, they do not experience them at the same rate. Children's rates of development can be quite idiosyncratic; therefore, if your child is not completing some task at a similar rate as your neighbor's child or your niece or nephew, there is not necessarily something awry. In most instances, children are in control of the rate and pacing of their development.

Theorist Richard Gentry identified five stages of spelling and writing development through which most children progress, more or less sequentially. In this chapter, we will discuss two of the stages specifically. The others will be introduced in subsequent chapters that are more directly relevant.

The first stage of writing and spelling development (referred to as the *precommunicative stage*) involves scribble writing. Scribble writing can potentially prove irritating to the parent who routinely finds books, bills, and important papers that prominently display the scribblings of the toddler. But it is significant and essential to your child's natural development as a writer. Scribble writing signifies that your child knows that writing is symbolic, it means something, and it is an important aspect of communication.

As your child advances (in respect to age and development), you will notice that her or his writing increases in sophistication. You might notice that the child uses one, two, or three letters to represent a word. This trait would be characteristic of the second stage known as the *semiphonetic*.

So, at this point, you might be wondering about ways in which you can assist in the development of your child's writing. First of all, you can provide tools for writing without breaking your bank. For little cost, you can stock up on different types of paper, crayons, pencils, pens, and markers. With young children (toddlers and preschoolers), their fine motor skills, such as the ability to hold small items well, and eye-hand coordination might not be as well-developed as slightly older children, for example, those in the early elementary grades. Thus, it becomes important to obtain large writing utensils that they can easily manipulate.

Also, provide opportunities for writing. Such an opportunity might be as simple as helping your child practice writing her or his name. Yet, be careful here; the goal is to provide the child an opportunity to develop writing ability, not to achieve perfection.

Parents and caregivers can also furnish chances to write by using young children's desire to help for their collective advantage. Young children like to feel as if they are capable and useful. They love it when we make them feel as if their help has been invaluable. Build on this strength and help them to develop their writing skills simultaneously by asking them to help you write the family's grocery list. Give your child a sheet of paper and ask her or him to write down groceries that are needed as you dictate the list. If you find that memory will not serve you, transcribe your child's writing onto a separate sheet of paper or ask for his permission to do so in parentheses next to his writing.

Although it seems like an insignificant point, allow your child to sign her name on cards and notes rather than doing it for her. Further, encourage your child to write notes, telephone messages, thank-you notes, and letters (even if they appear illegible to you). You can always add a transcription to the original.

As we discussed in relation to both speaking and reading, provide your child with opportunities to see you engaged in writing and share your writing with your child. If you are writing a letter, read the child an age-appropriate excerpt, or if someone has extended a courtesy to you or your family, take your child along to select a thank-you card and involve her or him in the writing of the note.

Lastly, you should be cognizant of the fact that there is a connection between writing proficiency and being read to. In a study of early readers (cited in Morrow's *Literacy Development in the Early Years: Helping*

Children Read and Write), it was determined that there were certain traits that were common in the homes of those children identified as early readers. The traits included:

- parents/caregivers who read to them;
- parents/caregivers who readily assisted with reading/writing tasks;
- parents/caregivers who served as reading/writing role models;
- books (either owned or borrowed) were present in their homes;
- reading and writing materials were found throughout the home; and
- children were frequently taken to the library.

Chapter 6

Selecting a School

> When you control a man's thinking you do not have to worry about his actions. You do not have to tell him not to stand here or go yonder. He will find his "proper place" and he will stay in it. You do not need to send him to the back door. He will go without being told. In fact, if there is no back door, he will cut one for his special benefit. His education makes it necessary.
> —Carter G. Woodson, Historian and Educator
> (*The Mis-Education of the Negro*)

The preschool years bring a vast array of new challenges for parents and caregivers. One of the most prominent might be the selection of an appropriate educational setting. Most of us (regardless of circumstance) want the best for our children and that includes the best education.

I believe that very few examples display this parental concern for children's educational success more poignantly than an example presented in Denny Taylor and Catherine Dorsey-Gaines's *Growing Up Literate: Learning from Inner-City Families* (1988). In the book outlining a study completed, the authors introduced a young, single mother who was living with her two children in an abandoned building. The family's health and safety were constantly in peril. Yet, the mother (given the pseudonym Tanya) engaged her children in literacy activities in the home, checked her daughter's homework, and did as much as she could to ensure that the child remained successful in her first-grade class.

This example eloquently shows that socioeconomic stability is not a corollary to parental concern or value of education. In fact, many parents of color *know* that education is the only means of class mobility that their children potentially have.

Although the task of finding an appropriate school is stressful for any parent, distinct dilemmas are posed for the parents or caregivers of children of color. A major issue surrounding the selection of an appropriate educational site for this group of parents involves *trust*. Whereas we can offer our children protection and inculcate them with our values within our respective homes, can we trust others with those responsibilities as our children step out into the "real world?" As a parent who has recently been involved in this process, I clearly understand the dilemma and its accompanying anxiety.

Lack of trust in school systems can be the aftermath of a variety of experiences. Parents' educational experiences while growing up can engender this type of distrust. The belief that schools and social service agencies are too closely linked, bureaucratic, or racist can also prompt feelings of suspicion and uncertainty, as can the experience of attempting to get help for a child with special needs.

One rather unfortunate outcome of distrust has been the rise in the number of families home-schooling their children. There are difficulties attached to this decision, even though it remains an individual choice. First, a number of Euro-American parents who do not want their children exposed to people of color or learning about them have chosen this route. Additionally, there are strict legal guidelines for home-schooling of which many parents are unaware. Further, it might not prove cost-effective for single-parent families or families that rely on the incomes of both parents. Lastly, at some point, the child that you have home-schooled will encounter the dilemmas associated with the American educational system and society in general. It simply becomes a matter of time.

For those who decide that it proves worthwhile to at least investigate the schools available, serious thought should be given to the educational arena in which your children will plausibly enter.

THE PROCESS OF FINDING THE RIGHT SCHOOL

The first step in the process of selecting an appropriate educational setting involves clarifying your values about education. What is important to you, educationally?

Some parents might prefer an Afrocentric setting, a place in which students and teachers are Black and the curriculum is reflective of African-centered values. Afrocentric schools sometimes prove more beneficial to Black youngsters than schools that would be considered multiracial, multicultural, or predominantly Euro-American. For instance, research suggests that older Black students do better academically, socially, and personally at historically Black colleges and universities than they do at those characterized as predominantly White.

The value in Afrocentric schools is derived primarily from *cultural synchronization*, a term used by Jacqueline Jordan Irvine in her book *Black Students and School Failure* (1991). Cultural synchronization, according to Irvine, is based on the principle that Blacks share a specific culture and exhibit certain cultural attributes, such as a value of genuine personal expression and a social orientation to time. Although I can acknowledge the benefit for some of Afrocentric schools, I find the definition of specific cultural attributes, such as social time orientation, problematic. In my estimation, these attributes become stereotypic and essentialist when used by the wrong people.

Others caregivers might value settings that are multiracial and a curriculum that reflects a respect for multicultural diversity and cultural acceptance. I would state that such schools could best be considered few and far between. In spite of the fact that we live during an era in which de jure segregation has been outlawed, schools remain segregated, de facto. The American public school system can be characterized as two separate and unequal school systems; one existing for the poor and those of color, the other serving the children of middle-class, White America.

That leads to a discussion of the last choice. Unfortunately, some parents and caregivers are aware of a harsh reality. In many instances, settings that are predominantly White receive more than their fair share of educational resources and offer their students a greater variety of programs and services. Thus, this group of parents might feel more comfortable choosing predominantly White school settings for their children.

Ultimately, this decision is a personal one. Furthermore, it is not necessarily permanent. You can always change your position. Be mindful of a lesson that I am slowly learning. You will *not* find everything that you desire in any one specific educational setting. But you should be able to find the bulk of that which you seek and live with or supplement that which is not provided. Of paramount importance is your child's personal and educational needs, as well as her level of comfort in the educational setting selected.

Other issues to determine ahead include whether you are interested in having your child attend a public, private, or religious setting. How convenient are school and daycare hours and locations? How much are you able to comfortably afford? If the response to the last question is not much, there is no need to worry. You are still entitled to a premium education (as determined by you) for your child. Whether your child is enrolled in a Headstart program or local daycare, she or he is entitled to the *very best* the setting has to offer. It is up to you, however, to ensure that the best is received.

The next step involved is to call and arrange visits to prospective schools or classes that your child will attend.

Under the next subheading, readers will find that much of the information provided pertains to those settings that are multiracial or predominantly White. Although Afrocentric settings pose a unique set of challenges, the two aforementioned settings often pose a number of difficulties regarding the representation of people from traditionally marginalized cultures and issues concerning cross-cultural, interpersonal exchange. My expertise lies in navigating such systems.

SCHOOL AND CLASS VISITS— THE PHYSICAL ENVIRONMENT

Under optimal circumstances, you (as your child's parents or caregivers) should visit prospective schools and classes. If an emergency or crisis arises, however, a trusted family member or friend may be sent with a list of your questions and concerns. Please make certain that whoever visits, arrives punctually. It is also important to carry paper and pen with you, so that notes may be taken. Because many of you will visit more than one site, it will become increasingly important to take good notes. Memory often proves less effective than we want to believe. Some of the questions that follow were modified from Louise Derman-Sparks's *Anti-Bias Curriculum: Tools for Empowering Young Children*.

On entering the facility, examine the outside structure and the entrance procedures. Are the school grounds well maintained? How easy is it to enter? Is a guard or school personnel seated at the entrance? Are children and parents greeted by name as they enter the school building? Are you (as a visitor) asked to sign in and display appropriate identification?

Once you are inside the building, examine walls and bulletin boards. Are children's work and drawings prominently displayed? Do wall hangings and decorations seem racially diverse? Do you see information or pictures reflective of your child's culture displayed? Is there a lot of student traffic in the halls? Do students seem actively engaged as you pass learning centers and classrooms? What is your general sense of the environment? Do school personnel make an attempt to assist you in finding your destination?

As you enter your child's prospective classroom or learning center, is your presence acknowledged? Even if the teacher is engaged with students, your presence should be recognized, since you made an appointment and should have been expected. If you are told that there will be a slight wait, use your time wisely. Ask the teacher if it would be permissible for you to look around. Conversely, if the teacher is ready to begin, ask if it would be all right for you to look around at the end of the visit. As you continue reading, you will be able to determine that it is essential to make the most of every moment of your visit.

As you examine the classroom, once again examine walls and bulletin boards for student work and drawings, in addition to wall hangings and decorations that are racially diverse and inclusive of your child's racial or cultural background. Are there posters that emphasize a love of learning and literacy? Is the classroom colorful and inviting, or drab and uninspiring?

Peruse class libraries. Is the library area inviting and neat? Are books in good condition? As you look through the available books, do you see racially diverse characters? Do you see characters and real-life figures who appear Black? Do books feature current copyright dates and include racial or ethnic terms that are current? For instance, I am certain that you would not want your child reading a book that described her or him as a "Negro" in the 1990s. Is there a preponderance of books featuring animals as story protagonists? Are both male and female characters portrayed as active and taking leadership roles? Do you recognize any of the book titles?

Examine play areas, as well. Are there art materials (e.g., paints, play dough, crayons, markers) that reflect diverse skin shades (including those that are brown)? Are there pictures of different types of families and genders completing a variety of household chores? Are dolls and small figures racially and ethnically diverse and representative of both genders? Are there dolls that are anatomically correct?

CLASSROOM INTERPERSONAL RELATIONS

Although the school or classroom's physical environment will send a definite message about the way in which children (generally), children of color (specifically), and the community in which the school appears are valued, it is equally important to examine the way in which adult school personnel interact with children and the way in which children treat other children. Be mindful that your child will spend a lot of time in that particular environment, if it is selected. Also, keep in mind that facades are not easily maintained. If you observe carefully, you will get a sense of what lies beneath the surface.

Are the teacher and other adults in the classroom actively involved with *all* the children? Does the teacher respond to children's questions or concerns with interest and enthusiasm or nonchalance and sarcasm? You will be able to distinguish between enthusiasm that is feigned and that which seems authentic. Does the teacher appear excessively negative or punitive?

Do you sense that the teacher is genuinely concerned about *all* the children? Do you get the sense that the teacher views students as deficient and needing a lot of work? Do you witness preferential treatment as it pertains to race? ethnicity? gender? How do the teacher and other adults speak to children? Is the classroom a busy and exciting place to be?

In regard to student-to-student interaction, how do children respond to each other? Do they appear cooperative or competitive? Do they seem to have to vie for the teacher's attention and affections? Do some children appear targeted and mistreated by the others? How do they talk to each other? How are student disagreements settled?

YOUR INTERVIEW WITH THE TEACHER

Usually, teachers will introduce themselves and tell you a little about their school settings or respective classrooms. As you sit down for your interview with the teacher, be assertive and be clear about what you want for your child, educationally and personally. This task should not prove daunting, as you gave serious thought to such matters ahead of your visit.

Introduce yourself. Share a little about the child who will possibly attend the setting, your expectations for your child, and of school personnel. As clearly as possible, convey your love and concern for your child and your desire that she or he receive the best possible education. Be cognizant of the fact that throughout your child's educational career, you will be the most effective advocate she or he has.

Inform the teacher early on that you wish to work in partnership with the school and teacher toward your child's educational success. Ultimately, you want the teacher to remember you and be aware that, if you decide on that setting, your presence will definitely be felt. As a former teacher I have told many, human nature alone ensures that a teacher is going to address the needs of those children whose parents are a continual presence *first*, even though her or his concern for the other children might be just as great.

Ask questions! How many adults are usually on site? In your child's potential learning center? What is the teacher-student ratio? How many certified teachers are there? What is the school's or teacher's educational philosophy? Philosophy on literacy development? How are content areas such as mathematics, science, and social studies approached? Does the school have an arts program that focuses on music, physical development, and fine arts?

At the end of the interview, request application forms, appropriate pamphlets, and brochures. Determine registration dates and times, as well as school hours and fees (if any). Remain noncommittal and thank the teacher for her or his time. Follow-up with a personally written thank-you note. Remember, you have other sites to explore, and even if you do not, it is not necessary to inform the teacher of this.

The last step in the process is the most difficult. With all the information at your fingertips, your notes, and memories, now you must decide.

It might seem as if most of this information is directed toward parents who have the financial resources to pick and choose the appropriate school for their youngsters. What about those parents who don't feel as if they have a great deal of choice? For whatever reason, there might be only one school from which this group of parents might choose. Yet, there is choice even within restriction. There are different classes and instructors from which you might choose. You are not required to merely *accept* the class or learning center that the school determines best for your child. You make the final decision and for that reason, it is important to take a proactive stance. Examine the school, the classes available to your child, and meet with your child's potential teachers.

Whatever the school setting, you as a parent or caregiver must make it work for you and that task requires that you are *vigilant, observant,* and *prepared to assume your role as educational advocate for your child.*

Chapter 7

Early Elementary School Readers and Writers

> I have often reflected upon the new vistas that reading opened to me. I knew right there in prison that reading had changed forever the course of my life. As I see it today, the ability to read awoke inside me some long dormant craving to be mentally alive.
> —Malcolm X, Political Activist
> (*The Autobiography of Malcolm X as told to Alex Haley*)

As your child's first tutor, you have worked diligently to facilitate the development of her or his language and literacy capabilities. Children begin learning about language and literacy, as well as the world surrounding them, from birth. They learn through exposure and the utilization of skills they are learning. They do *not* develop such qualities through the use of drills and worksheets. This point should be remembered as your child continues to acquire literacy skills in the context of a formal classroom.

This chapter begins with the basic premise that your child (ranging from grades K–2) is now consistently attending school and receiving beginning reading and writing instruction.

CAPABILITIES OF THE CHILD ENTERING PRIMARY SCHOOL

By the time children reach five or six years of age, they have approximately 2,500 words in their expressive vocabulary repertoires and are able to understand many more words. They, generally, enter the formal school system with basic understandings of print, sizable vocabularies, general commands of language, and internalized comprehension of grammatical rules.

In respect to books, your child (like many five-and six-year-olds) will enter the kindergarten or first-grade classroom with a knowledge of book print, mechanical and form concepts (e.g., letters, words, sentences, punctuation), orientation and directionality (reading from left to right and front to back), and story sense (understanding that books have plots, characters, settings, and so forth).

Your child's writing may also show signs of sophistication. Referring back to Gentry's stages of invented spelling, your child might have reached the developmental level called the *phonetic stage*. During this stage, occurring after the *precommunicative* and *semiphonetic* stages, your child's writing will reflect all the essential sounds. In other words, most children at this stage of writing development will spell words the way they sound.

Another point of writing sophistication is frequently witnessed in children who have been read to on a regular basis. There is a suggested correlation between writing proficiency and being read to. For this group of children, their writing (according to their translations of their stories) contains elements of the stories that have been read to them. For instance, if one analyzes stories written by children who routinely enjoy fairy tales, one should discover that their stories frequently begin with "once upon a time," include royalty, or end with "they lived happily ever after." This phenomenon is known as *intertextuality*.

Your child will bring a number of strengths to the classroom. They include learnings about language, literacy, her or his culture, and the world. Students potentially bring a rich diversity of experience to the classroom, which has traditionally been discounted.

The contemporary view of children and the significant role that families and communities play in literacy development directly contrasts a more traditional notion that children enter classrooms as blank slates, or tabulae rasae (a term coined by philosopher John Locke). This belief seems to disregard the substantial contribution of forces (e.g., parents, caregivers, community-based institutions) other than the school in the education and socialization of children.

Brazilian educator Paulo Freire referred to this type of education as the "banking method." Students serve as empty repositories; the omniscient teacher fills these empty vessels. With the "banking method," the focus is on student deficit (that which students do not know) rather than student strength (that which they know).

At this point, some readers might be saying, "Yes, I have actively participated in my child's literacy development and will continue. I am cognizant of the potential strengths my child brings to the classroom. But when does my child begin to read autonomously? What role should the school be expected to play in my child's development as a beginning reader and writer?"

IS THERE SOMETHING WRONG? I'VE DONE EVERYTHING RIGHT AND MY CHILD STILL ISN'T READING?

Whereas most parents and caregivers seem to accept that children learn to speak naturally, they appear overcome by feelings of anxiety when their children reach five or six years of age and have not started to read independently. If their respective children are not reading autonomously and with great interest, they become anxious that "there is something wrong."

Clarification is needed on a few essential points. First of all, there is no requisite age to read. During the 20th century, it has been commonly accepted that six years is the age at which most children are "ready" to read. But for all intents and purposes, such a determination is an arbitrary one.

It seems that the specified age can be traced back to the early 1920s. In 1925, developmental psychologist Arnold Gesell advocated maturation as the most consequential factor in reading acquisition. In 1931, researchers Morphett and Washburne supported the postponement of reading instruction until a child was developmentally "old enough." A study completed by the duo indicated that children with a mental age of six years and six months were more successful on reading achievement tests than younger children.

Yet, when analyzing scientific studies claiming to measure intelligence and academic progress (especially earlier ones in comparison with those categorized as relatively current), one should be conscious that such studies were routinely conducted using groups *reflective of the norm.* White and middle-class children were, most likely, the subjects. Children of color were not, generally, included in such pools because of a perpetuated racist mythology, which deemed them intellectually inferior.

The second point of clarification focuses on the point that, in reiteration, children develop at their own pace. Each child's development is idiosyncratic. No two children develop at the same time or in the same fashion. It takes faith in your efforts, as a parent and a literacy mentor, to assist your child in literacy development. If you have started early and implemented some of the suggestions included in this book, you should have little doubt that your child *will* read.

The final observation to be made on this matter involves our seemingly national obsession with diagnosis and learning disability. It is clearly understood that there are children who are reading disabled or learning disabled. Early intervention can sometimes assist this group of children in attaining educational success. Far too frequently, however, children are labeled very early in their academic careers as disabled and perceive themselves as failures or "stupid." More plausible reasons for delay in literacy development might include insufficient time for appropriate progress, lack of exposure, or opportunities to succeed. This frenzy to classify is even further exacerbated for children of color, and it can have more deleterious effects for them.

Your child should be provided adequate time and opportunity to develop as a reader and writer and spared your anxiety. Very little can have a more harmful effect than an overanxious parent "pushing" a child to advance before she or he is ready. In many such instances, the "push" is concentrated on the parent's needs more so than those of the child.

Learning more about the way in which beginning literacy development is approached in your child's school would, also, prove advantageous. In this way, you and your child's teacher work more effectively together. You avoid serving cross-purposes. As a parent or caregiver, you should actively work toward establishing an educational *partnership* with your child's teacher and other school personnel to ensure your child's optimal academic success.

HOW IS BEGINNING READING AND WRITING INSTRUCTION APPROACHED IN SCHOOLS TODAY?

After viewing a few homework assignments that children bring home, many parents come to the realization that things have changed since they went to school.

Numerous educational innovations have been implemented and schools are constantly working to upgrade the services they provide to students and their families. Educational innovations appear cyclical in nature. They seem to shift back and forth between extremes that could best be characterized as liberal, progressive, or back-to-basics. These shifts are often prompted by phenomena occurring outside the realm of education. For instance, political shifts, the demands of industry, nationalistic competition, as well as new research developments on the brain and human development have all affected the type and level of instruction that children within the United States receive. Innovations and cycles are mentioned because they have also affected the way in which beginning reading and writing is approached in U.S. schools.

Since the advent of education and schooling in the United States, two philosophies about reading instruction have dominated. One philosophy places meaning-making at the center of the effective teaching of reading. The other focuses upon letter-sound correspondence and decoding as central to the development of a proficient reader.

In its current form, this long-standing and cyclical battle over the best approach to teaching beginning reading and writing has taken the form of the Whole Language-Phonics debate. This debate has received a great deal of attention from educators, policymakers, and the mainstream media during the past 15 years.

WHAT IS WHOLE LANGUAGE?

Whole Language received its genesis in New Zealand, traveled through England and Canada, and reached the United States as a grassroots movement introduced by teachers rather than administrative policy mandate. In respect to definition, Whole Language is a *philosophy* about teaching, learning, and literacy development. It is based on the belief that reading and writing develop naturally, just as speaking and listening do. Teachers in such classrooms serve as facilitators; they guide and support children's learning. They lead their students from dependence to autonomy.

In a Whole Language classroom, there is no one *right* way to do anything. Children are allowed to move at their own distinctive paces. Teachers are trained to appreciate student difference rather than hastily identify student deficit. Children are viewed as people with varied interests, delights, fears, strengths, and weaknesses. There is a focus on and respect for the whole child. An atmosphere, comfortable and inviting of risk-taking, is established for the novice reader and writer.

Within the context of Whole Language classrooms, there are some features that are common. These features include:

- Children reading everyday and at various intervals during the day.
- Children reading authentic literature (real books) for real purposes.
- Children writing everyday, throughout the day.
- Children using a process approach to writing.
- Children using time in a fluid, but structured, manner.

As easily determined by the description, the emphasis of Whole Language is meaning-centered, ensuring that literacy activities are meaningful to learners. This is a tremendous shift from the boring worksheets, overly structured reading and writing lessons, and Dick and Jane readers with which many parents are familiar.

Yet, in spite of its many positive attributes, Whole Language has proved a public relations nightmare for its advocates, and it has been unfairly declared a failure in states such as California. Some of the initial public relations fallout resulted from the lack of clarity among proponents about the need for and role of decoding and comprehension strategies within Whole Language. Initially, there were Whole Language advocates who stated that there was no need for the explicit teaching of skills for beginning readers.

Another camp of supporters espoused the view that Whole Language and the explicit teaching of reading skills were not mutually exclusive, as long as the teaching of such skills did not occur in the same excessively systematic and meaningless fashion that it did in the past.

Critics of Whole Language were concerned about the role of explicit teaching, as well. For this group, Whole Language proved not much more than a "feel-good, anything goes" approach to teaching and learning. But how did children learn to read autonomously without being taught to decode and understand letter-sound correspondence?

This concern loomed especially large for those concerned about Black children who are poor and (probably) bidialectical, as well as those children who are bilingual. Educators, such as Lisa Delpit, were concerned that, without the explicit teaching of skills, children categorized as bidialectical would remain at a disadvantage when they entered society and the world of work. Without necessary literacy skills, they would remain disempowered and extant social stratification would be reinforced.

Others, concerned more specifically with the welfare of bilingual learners, worried that it would prove especially difficult for those speaking other languages to decipher the English language, in all of its complexity. With its Germanic base, English has many irregular rules and uses that might not be aptly grasped without formal instruction.

Other difficulties with Whole Language resulted from inadequate teacher preparation. There were numbers of teachers across the country who received little if any training in Whole Language, but they were expected to successfully implement it in their classrooms. This situation could best be characterized as a Catch-22.

Additionally, many school districts reported that there was less emphasis on standardized testing in the lower elementary grades. Many teachers were expected to use Whole Language-based activities while being evaluated for successfully teaching-to-the-test. A number of teachers, especially those working in urban centers, knew that their jobs were dependent on students' achievement, as determined by standardized test scores. Thus, using Whole Language strategies was considered an exercise in futility. Teachers knew that standardized testing *was* inconsistent and incongruent with Whole Language philosophy and practice.

Although never fully given a chance to succeed, Whole Language was officially declared a failure by some states during the early 1990s.

WHAT IS PHONICS?

There was once a time when large numbers of children entered the primary school classroom without knowing the alphabet. Today, knowing the alphabet is the rule rather than the exception. There is more than one reason for this change, but the role of educational television cannot be ignored. For example, with the advent of *Sesame Street* in 1969, most children entering school were quite familiar with the alphabet and numbers one through ten. Resultantly, many beginning reading programs no longer commenced with the alphabet. Instead, these programs started by teaching the sounds corresponding to specific letters.

Understanding the connection between letters and sounds is one of the building blocks of reading decoding. According to reading experts, such as Jeanne Chall, an emphasis on *phonics* and the development of reading subskills (in the early grades) leads to the development of a more proficient reader in the upper grades. But what exactly is phonics?

According to Professor of Reading Dorothy Strickland, in her book *Teaching Phonics Today: A Primer for Educators* (1998), *phonics* refers to "instruction in the sound-letter relationship used in reading and writing. It involves an understanding of the alphabetic principle (. . . relationship between spoken sounds and letters or combinations of letters) on which the English language is based and a knowledge of the sounds associated with a particular letter or combination of letters" (p. 5).

Yet, knowledge of phonological relationships is only one of the decoding skills and strategies employed by proficient readers. Such readers also demonstrate phonemic awareness (the ability to segment words for phonics or spelling); structural analysis (the ability to use word parts, e.g., prefixes, suffixes, and roots) to establish meaning; and self-correcting techniques, among others.

Advocates of phonics-based instruction boast of the numerous studies completed that suggest a strong correlation between phonics instruction and reading proficiency. Yet, while some of the alleged "evidence" is compelling, many of the studies rely on the results of standardized testing. Such testing, from its inception, has been shown to privilege knowledge that is Eurocentric, mainstream, and middle class. It has been historically biased against those from most traditionally marginalized cultures, as well as second-wave U.S. immigrants.

Conversely, Whole Language has established a different way of thinking about teaching, learning, literacy, and (even) testing. As such, it would prove incompatible to test its successes using standardized testing. In many ways, comparing two philosophies or *approaches* that are so vastly different is inherently unfair. The word *approaches* is highlighted because those in both camps claim that Whole Language and phonics are not approaches, but many educators refer to them as such.

Today, innovations make phonics instruction accessible and interesting for children. Phonics programs, such as Project R.E.A.D. and the Open Court series, can offer children tactile (touching) ways of learning the alphabet, introduce mnemonic devices (for easy memorization of rules), and acquaint children with quality children's literature. Phonics instruction, however, has a long-standing history of being tedious, excessively time-consuming, and punitive, especially for those readers having difficulty grasping initial concepts, as well as those students considered advanced.

Traditionally, through phonics, students (regardless of their initial level of reading proficiency) were directly taught letter-sound correspondence through whole-class instruction. Phonics lessons were reinforced with worksheets and basal readers that contained controlled vocabulary (certain words appeared with great frequency according to the sound being learned at the time). Another unfortunate outcome resulting from this approach to teaching and use of basal readers was the proliferation of ability-grouping in reading instruction. The concept behind ability-grouping is that children are placed in small, homogeneous groups for the purpose of tailoring their instruction to meet their needs. Difficulties with ability-grouping usually center around the following points: Such groups are customarily fixed for the course of the academic year, meaning that students generally remain in the same groups; groups are based on student deficit, the skills students do not have; and children placed in low-ability groups are stigmatized by the value judgments resulting from their placements.

One of the most problematic concerns raised about ability-grouping, however, is that children have traditionally been grouped according to the teacher's perception of the student's reading ability. Although teacher decision-making on this issue was frequently influenced by standardized tests scores, researchers (e.g., Ray Rist) suggested that teachers (regardless of race) more frequently based these decisions about student ability on such factors as dress, absence of body odor, skin color, cleanliness, linguistic ability, and perceptions of student's socioeconomic status or family background. In other words, teachers expected certain children to fail and that belief had very little to do with the student's ability.

Although the ramifications of such decision-making are vast, a key point is that teacher expectation often leads to *self-fulfilling prophecies.* Students, actually, begin to behave in ways that confirm teachers beliefs about them. Thus, if a teacher believes that a student will fail, the student will usually be treated in ways that contribute to her failure. Subsequently, the student will, most likely, fail.

Phonics instruction is, also, recurrently relied on as a panacea for a number of other problems within U.S. schools. Considered a back-to-basics "approach," phonics is brought back whenever more progressive measures are deemed failures. Even though phonics might be effective for some learners, it is habitually brought back for the wrong reasons.

Yet, what is the *best* approach to literacy development for children, generally? What is the *best* approach for Black children?

THE BEST APPROACH TO BEGINNING
READING AND WRITING INSTRUCTION
FOR BLACK CHILDREN

In relation to the Whole Language-phonics debate, the truth of the matter is that both arguments contain elements of validity. The dilemma lies in the espousing of any *one* philosophy as the best. Readers do not, exclusively, rely on either meaning-making or decoding skill.

Ken Goodman supports this statement's veracity. He declares that three systems rather than one help readers to make sense of printed material.

Goodman asserts that three cueing systems work interdependently to create reading proficiency. The systems include the *semantic system* (focusing on meaning), the *syntactic system* (emphasizing grammatical consistency), and the *graphophonic system* (targeting letter-sound correspondence). If all these systems are not working in concert, one is unable to read successfully.

While one philosophy and approach to literacy development might work for one learner, it could prove futile with another. A skilled teacher is able to use those instructional strategies and methods that meet the needs of each respective learner.

In my professional judgment, the best approach to literacy development in schools is one that is currently referred to as *balanced literacy instruction*. Balanced literacy instruction contains many elements of Whole Language, but it also teaches learners the skills and strategies required for reading proficiency and effective decoding.

Within a classroom that is reflective of balanced literacy instruction, exposure to reading is essential. Authentic children's literature and other "real" reading materials (such as magazines, newspapers) are present in the classroom. Students should be provided with "shared reading" opportunities, during which stories are shared with children in a relaxed environment. They are encouraged to read along with the teacher, as well as independently. Book print conventions and graphophonic concepts are reinforced.

Children read and write everyday, throughout the day. In respect to writing, children learn basic writing concepts. Additionally, they are given chances to creatively express themselves through writing.

Student creativity is fostered in the balanced literacy instruction classroom. The teacher does not rely on standardized test scores for grouping and assessment. Instead, a more flexible and fluid approach to grouping is used. For example, if a group of seven are having difficulty with a particular skill or strategy, those seven are grouped and the teacher works with them until mastery is attained. On the other hand, if the entire class needs reinforcement of a strategy, the entire class receives assistance until the skill is mastered.

Measures, other than standardized tests, are used for the purpose of documenting student success. Teachers might use authentic assessment instruments such as reading running records, informal inventories, and portfolios in corroboration of their own personal assessments of student strength and progress.

This description will probably appear closely aligned to the prior one, illustrating a Whole Language classroom, but there is one clearly delineated difference. Students are taught essential reading and writing skills and strategies directly and as needed in this classroom. Most significant, skills and strategies are taught within a meaningful context rather than using boring worksheets and "dead" text.

In order to assess the type of reading and writing instruction your child receives in her or his early elementary classroom, it is best to visit, observe, and ask questions. In the process, not only will you learn about the way in which literacy development is approached in your child's respective classroom, you will also establish that you are an active participant in your child's education.

ESTABLISHING AN EDUCATIONAL PARTNERSHIP WITH YOUR CHILD'S TEACHER

Early in the academic year, you (as parent or caregiver) should arrange a time to visit your child's classroom and confer with her or his teacher. If possible, you might even wish to set up a schedule for volunteering in your child's learning center. While you receive a firsthand account of classroom happenings and atmosphere through your volunteer efforts, a fringe benefit involves your child's appreciation (sometimes gradual) of your presence and concern.

In relation to observations and conferences, however, initially establish that the visit is prompted by interest in your child rather than displeasure. Explain that you view such visits commonplace and as one of your responsibilities as a parent or guardian. At this point, you wish to refrain from establishing an adversarial relationship with the teacher, instead trying to build one of mutual trust and respect. Although this is your goal, the author realizes that, in some instances, the establishment of such a relationship is implausible for a number of reasons.

If you are unable to meet with your child's teacher, send notes and call. Explain the difficulty so that your absence is not perceived as a lack of concern for your child or her or his education. Yet, I would advise, quite strongly, that you make the time to visit your child's teacher at some point during the school year. Research suggests that parental involvement has a positive effect on students' academic success.

During your teacher-parent conference, share information about the literacy events in which your family engages in the home. If you read stories routinely, share the titles and suggest that the teacher read them in class. If your child writes creative stories, share details about the way in which your child approaches writing in your home.

In respect to cross-cultural exchanges with teachers, it is essential to share information about your culture and your family. In Chapter 1, current and projected teacher demographics, in addition to the paucity of teachers of color, were discussed. For the most part, the elementary teacher corps is predominantly White and female. Demographics suggest that this trend will continue.

Thus, it is plausible that your child will have teachers who could be considered *cultural outsiders*. Cultural outsiders are, most likely, unfamiliar with your culture. Such teachers may not have any personal interaction outside of the classroom with Blacks or people from other traditionally marginalized cultures. It is important to provide some details about your family and your heritage in an attempt to educate the teacher.

For example, if, after observing your child's class library, it becomes apparent that there are relatively few books featuring Blacks, other historically marginalized groups, topics associated with revisionist history, you might choose to offer titles that could be included. Possibly, it would prove more expedient to donate several such books to the library. Such improvements do not only prove useful to your child, they enrich the experience of *all* the children in the class. View suggestions as ways in which you are fulfilling your responsibility to all of the children in your child's classroom. The issue of multicultural children's literature will be more fully broached in the next chapter.

Also, take the opportunity to ask for clarification on classroom practices and homework procedures about which you are unclear. For example, how are children's reading and speech errors approached in the classroom? Does the teacher tell children that they are "wrong" or spend an excessive amount of time correcting spoken grammatical "errors?" Does the teacher lead children to correct their own errors? Are value judgments attached to student errors (e.g., the teacher making statements about children's use of "poor" or "improper" English)? According to the teacher, how should you deal with your child's errors at home? Also, if there is disagreement on the issue, be certain to ask for further clarification and suggested resources that can be read for additional information on the strategy indicated.

In regard to homework practices, a common dilemma for parents is posed by the classroom implementation of *inventive spelling,* a common feature of many early elementary (K–2) classrooms. Inventive spelling is when children write words phonetically (the way they sound rather than using standard spelling) initially. Many parents become quite upset with the practice because the technique has not been adequately explained to them. They view it as encouraging poor spelling and writing.

The purpose of inventive spelling, however, is to provide children greater latitude in writing, allow creativity to flow, and give them the opportunity to sound unfamiliar words out in an attempt to make sense of them. Parents fear that children will not be given standard spelling instruction and will spell in this fashion indefinitely. In an effectual classroom, inventive spelling is only commonplace from grades Kindergarten through 2, yet students are concurrently learning standard spelling and writing strategies.

If your child's teacher is encouraging inventive spelling, ask for recommendations on ways in which you might assist your child. If the child comes across an unfamiliar word, do you prompt him or her to sound it out? At what point, do you stop such a process? If the child expresses frustration, do you spell the word for him or her? What is the suggested approach?

HOW DO I CONTINUE ENHANCING MY CHILD'S LITERACY DEVELOPMENT IN MY HOME?

Your goal in the home is to *maintain* the interest in reading that you have already worked to inspire. Some parents decide to assist their children's teachers in beginning literacy development by purchasing mass-produced phonics workbooks from local bookstores or television infomercials.

Subsequently, they force the children to complete a specified number of pages. Although these parents do receive an A for effort, such attempts are misguided (at best). In spite of the fact that they believe that they are helping their children, this group of parents is doing more harm than good. Instead of fostering and maintaining a love of reading, the desire to read and enjoy books is being slowly stamped out. Children are learning that reading is boring and devoid of meaning. I do not believe that this message is the desired outcome.

A word of caution should also be offered about computer-assisted programs known as *tutorials* or *video worksheets*. Although many parents are impressed by these programs because they are high-tech, they do not provide much more than their paper predecessors. These tutorials are simply tools.

Many teachers receive extensive training on the teaching of beginning reading strategy and skills. They learn theory and ways in which to translate theory into effective practice. Workbooks and tutorials can never serve as acceptable substitutes for the expertise of a skilled teacher.

There is no need to supplement the teacher's efforts in this way if progress is being made, and you will be able to immediately identify progress. Does your child readily select books to read while at home? Does your child bring books home from school? Does the child make positive statements about her or his capabilities as a reader and writer? Does your youngster ask to visit the library? Does she or he make efforts to read to you, your partner, or siblings? As your child reads, does she or he make efforts to self-correct reading errors? Is your daughter able to write her own name? Is your youngster making the mental connections between writing and meaning? Does your child's writing display one or two letters that are written as words? Is your son attempting to sound out words that he is uncertain about (in respect to spelling)? Does he show interest in words?

If the response to the majority of these questions is yes, then progress is evident. Conversely, this book will provide suggestions for situations in which progress is not easily detected.

It is hoped that you will continue with those home-based literacy activities that have proved so successful in your home from your child's infancy through the preschool years. Your efforts might also reinforce your values about race, culture, and identity for your daughter or son.

As your child enters the arena of school, she might make a transition from a warm and loving home environment that proves supportive of her burgeoning race-conscious identity and cultural values to a school environment that is less affirming. Depending on the setting, your child might be receiving seemingly inadvertent messages about the societal importance of the mainstream, and invisibility or disrespect shown to people of color. While you strive toward working with the teacher to create a comfortable environment for all the children in the respective classroom, you should also stand to reinforce your child's positive sense of self and pride in her or his racial and cultural heritage. Simultaneously, you will want to counter a popular mainstream message that pride in one's own race and culture implies hatred for others.

Introduce literacy themes to your child. For example, you will still want to surround your child with positive images of Blackness in books as you did during toddlerhood. Yet, now you and your child might choose to read different books on Africa or the Caribbean. You might wish to explore the concept of family and define the term for yourselves. Have children interview different family members, living both near and far. Assist them in compiling the interviews and photographs in the form of a book. Such experiences prove memorable and meaningful to youngsters.

Relatedly, you might want to read about different types of families, addressing the fact that the binding feature of all families is love. Further, all families possess forms of strength and resilience. For Black families, this concept is especially important as concerted efforts were made to destroy our families, historically. Yet, we have adapted and survived, in spite of the odds. It might also prove beneficial to take your child on historic trips, to places that your family treasures, and to cultural events.

Another literacy strategy that might be introduced would be *parental letter-writing* to your child. Through letters that we write to our children, we are able to introduce and preserve family history for them, share special and specific details about their lives, and describe the tremendous impact of those details on our lives. Letters written to our children might provide them with a bit more insight regarding our identities, feelings, and personal reflections as human beings that extend beyond our role as parents.

The literacy development benefits of this activity include the fact that children appreciate reading materials that are personally meaningful and relevant to their lives. Children will also benefit from responding (in writing) to some of your letters.

Keep letters simple. Write in your natural voice and attempt to genuinely reveal your heart. Write at regular intervals. Place letters in unexpected places, such as under pillows, in lunch boxes, and in book bags.

Through your literacy development efforts, you are working to broaden your child's prior knowledge background, a component that is essential to reading proficiency, while concurrently reinforcing and further developing your child's positive, race-conscious identity.

Also, be prepared for your child to bring home tough questions about race, ethnicity, and culture. In some instances, your heart will ache as you discuss such issues. Yet, make the time to discuss them and offer (rather than push) books and readings that might supplement your discussion.

Chapter 8

❖❖❖

The Older Child and Literacy Development

> What is the role of the word—the spoken word, the preached word, the whispered-in-the-night-time word, the written word, the published word—in the fight for black freedom?
> —Vincent Harding (as quoted in Charles Lawrence's "The Word and the River: Pedagogy as Scholarship as Struggle")

In his book *How To Succeed in Business Without Being White,* publisher and chief executive officer of *Black Enterprise* magazine Earl Graves projects job growth during the millennium in three broad areas:

- outsourcing (independent companies that offer services conventionally rendered in-house by corporations and public entities);
- computer technology, telecommunications, multimedia software and on-line entertainment; and
- health care and other services for aging baby boomers.

The greatest opportunities will, presumably, be contained within the second category (computer technology, telecommunications, and others). Labor Bureau forecasters indicate that technicians will compose one-fifth of the workforce by 2005. The number of jobs in computer-related fields will increase by 90%.

Concomitantly, the federal government and corporate entities, that have typically relied on the labor of clerical staff, are downsizing and becoming more dependent on personal computers. Thus, Blacks who have traditionally held large numbers of clerical positions are being displaced. They are increasingly vulnerable to job elimination and employment insecurity.

Employment insecurity is further complicated as Blacks continue to be shut out of union-controlled industries, such as construction, and adversely affected by public policy decisions, such as term limits on welfare. These limits take recipients off welfare rolls, compelling them to work when sufficient employment opportunities for unskilled workers and childcare are virtually nonexistent. In spite of the fact that national unemployment rates have plummeted during recent years, not much has changed for some sectors of society.

Lack of opportunity for promotion and advancement also impede progress for Blacks. Without the increasingly complex literacy and computer skills required, a number of long-employed Black workers are placed in professional and economic jeopardy.

Projected job growth reports and issues of job elimination and lack of advancement are representative of economic and demographic shifts within U.S. society. The nation is rapidly transitioning from industry-based to one that is technologically advanced and undergirded by an information substructure. As society moves in this direction, societal literacy demands increase. Not only must workers be able to read text, they are also obligated to analyze, interpret, and process complex information. Further, they are expected to understand sophisticated computer technology with minimal assistance.

The desires for economic growth and potential class mobility, however, are not the only reasons for the development of advanced literacy skills among the Black populace. Enhanced literacy skills are also the means to social and political transformation. According to critical theorist Henry Giroux in his introduction to Paulo Freire and Donaldo Macedo's *Literacy: Reading the Word and the World*, "Literacy points to the need to develop an alternative discourse and critical reading of how ideology, culture and power work within late capitalist societies to limit, disorganize, and marginalize the more critical and radical everyday experiences and commonsense perceptions of individuals."

Historically, our people have understood the role that literacy plays in breaking the bonds of oppression (see Chapter 1) and obtaining political empowerment. The deprivation of literacy has been used strategically to maintain the institution of slavery and our enslavement and deny us the vote and our right to full democratic participation. Advanced literacy skills, including an individual's ability to critically evaluate text, assists us in understanding the intricate political codes that affect us and the interdependence of the global community to which we belong.

Placed within a historical framework, it seems that there has been a rift maintained within the Black community regarding the purpose of schools for African Americans and the greater importance of either economic or political empowerment. Although the debate seemed to begin in 1860 and reached a pinnacle during the first two decades of the 20th century, it remains alive even today.

Presently, the education that some Black youngsters, especially the poor and those living in urban centers and rural areas, receive in public schools proves to be an almost insurmountable disability. Independent studies conducted by Anyon, Leacock, and Popkewitz suggest that schools are assisting in the maintenance of society's political and economic status quo by educating students to remain in certain socioeconomic classes.

For example, in two of the studies (at least), it was suggested that schools serving lower socioeconomic school populations taught rote memorization, skill and drill instruction, and compliance with orders. In essence, it appears as if these students are being prepared for employment that requires the same types of skill. Conversely, upper-class populations were found to receive instruction that required the use of critical thinking and decision-making skills. Through the educations that they receive, poor youngsters are taught to accept the limited expectations that society holds for them, as well as their future roles as the politically impotent.

In spite of the fact that computer technology is becoming one of the fastest growing industries in the world, there are still children in the United States who will not see nor have access to computers during their Kindergarten through grade 12 educations. Data also suggest qualitative differences in respect to computer use for poor youngsters and those of color. It has been suggested that although students of color use the computer in school primarily for drill and practice, more affluent youngsters (particularly males) learn programming.

Limited access to knowledge secures the widening line of bifurcation between middle-class Blacks and those who are poor, as well as the colossal divide separating the poor of all races and this country's White elite. Limited access to knowledge can reinforce a docile and apathetic underclass. It additionally sustains the political and economic disenfranchisement of some sectors of the Black community.

The prevailing role of schools should be to assist students in gaining the literacy skills needed for optimal future success and the guarantee of *choice* in life options. Since your child should now have acquired basic literacy skills in the early elementary grades, she should be actively engaged in the development of the critical literacy skills needed for personal, social, political, and economic transformation during the upper elementary three through six grade years.

WHAT ARE THE ESSENTIAL COMPONENTS OF CRITICAL LITERACY DEVELOPMENT IN THE UPPER ELEMENTARY CLASSROOM?

Upper elementary grade youngsters should have numerous opportunities to hone the advanced literacy skills needed in today's increasingly complex society. In the classroom, there should be constant exposure to quality children's literature, a comprehensive understanding of connections between literacy and thinking, and interdisciplinary teaching and learning.

EXPOSURE TO QUALITY CHILDREN'S LITERATURE

One of the ways in which children become proficient readers is to read a wide variety of materials on a consistent basis. Studies suggest strong correlations between reading volume and increased vocabularies, growth in verbal skills, and knowledge acquisition. In an effort to provide consistent reading opportunities, teachers should furnish children with a regular diet of quality children's literature that is inclusive of multicultural selections.

Children's literature distinguishes itself from children's books with its high literary and artistic quality. Although children's literature can be viewed as both artistic creation and informational, it should also be viewed as political. Critic Isabelle Jan identified the integration of the child into society as a notable aim of children's literature. Therefore, the following deduction can be made: In conjunction with other societal forces, children's literature can serve as a powerful influence in shaping young minds and creating perceptions about the world in which we live.

Unfortunately, the children's literature commonly presented in schools is customarily representative of European and mainstream values. One plausible explanation for this phenomenon focuses on the fact that teachers often select the books with which they are most familiar. Routinely, they make literature selections for their classes, based on their perusal of lists (those distributed by the school or district primarily), the recollections of books they enjoyed as children, or those introduced to them during their academic careers. As a result, it appears almost standard fare for children to read White's *Charlotte's Web*, Milne's *Winnie the Pooh* or Sendak's *Where the Wild Things Are* during their school years (at least once), regardless of their respective interests or lives.

Although there is nothing wrong with exposing children to these classics, they should also be exposed to books that represent the views, perceptions, and life experiences of people of color and other marginalized groups within society. This representation is often achieved through multicultural children's literature.

What is multicultural children's literature, specifically? According to Violet Harris, in her edited collection *Teaching Multicultural Literature in Grades K–8*, the following definition is proposed:

> Multicultural literature refers to literature that focuses on people of color—African, Asian, Hispanic, and Native American; religious minorities, such as the Amish or Jewish; regional cultures, for example Appalachian and Cajun; the disabled; and the aged. To some extent, the term encompasses literature that presents women and girls in a multitude of roles that are not gender stereotyped. The element common to each group member is its marginal status and its lack of participation in "mainstream" organizations.

Such books should also contain positive, complex, and authentic portrayals of group members. It is insufficient to present large volumes of books that merely include characters or real-life figures from the varied groups in tangential roles. The characterizations presented in multicultural literature should be substantive and reflective of distinct cultural values.

Reading multicultural children's literature proves beneficial to children from marginalized groups in numerous ways. Primarily, it presents an accurate portrait of the world. We do not live in a monocultural society. The contributions of numerous groups and cultures have shaped civilization. As such, we should all be represented. Second, the positive, race-conscious identity of children from traditionally marginalized groups is reinforced as they experience positive, complex portrayals of themselves in books on a frequent basis. Such experiences can only serve to enhance these children's desire to read.

Far too routinely, however, the benefits of multicultural children's literature appear limited to its advantages for children of color. Euro-American children also gain from this literature. Through literature that is representative of society's full diversity, mainstream children may receive the message that the experiences of other groups within society are significant. They might also be relieved of a narrow, ethnocentric understanding of the world in which Europe and mainstream values are both primary and central. Instead, they might realize that the perspective of Euro-Americans is only one valid way of viewing the world. People of color also offer valid perspectives, knowledge, and experiences.

Harris states that teachers should not be forced into using multicultural children's literature in the classroom because compulsion could potentially prompt negative feelings about the books or groups represented. Aware of the research done on the effects of multicultural education, I find Harris's point a valid one. Yet, I also ardently believe that, as Blacks, we are often made to feel that we should not ask for that to which mainstream groups believe they are entitled. I additionally value Frederick Douglass's famous quote, "Power concedes nothing without demand."

It is the *right* of all Black children to receive an equitable education, in which they, like children from other traditionally marginalized cultures, see representations of themselves and their cultures that are fairly and positively drawn and realistically complex.

Teachers should be strongly encouraged to use such literature that benefits all the children within the classroom. If you, as a parent or caregiver, notice that the selections read and offered in your child's classroom are monocultural, it would probably prove advantageous to confer with your child's teacher in a nonconfrontational manner and encourage her to diversify class reading selections. It might also prove helpful to present a few recommended titles.

Be mindful that the input you contribute in your child's early elementary classroom makes a significant difference in his performance. Your active role in your child's academic progress and presence in his respective classroom remain as important currently as it did in the past.

Within the context of the classroom, children should also receive regular opportunities to interact with different genres (or types) of literature. Teachers should present children with chances to read folk tales, fables, fantasy, poetry, fiction, historical fiction, biography, autobiography, and expository (informational) books. Students should also get varied chances to read books (whole texts) rather than having all reading selections assigned from a literature anthology or basal reader.

Exposure to different authors, styles of writing, and genres will assist children in comprehending that different types of print materials are arranged in different manners. Diverse text types also require diverse approaches and modes of thought.

CONNECTIONS BETWEEN LITERACY AND THINKING

Literacy acquisition is a complex and active process. While engaged in literacy, one is engaged in the process of thought and meaning-making. Within the upper elementary grade classroom, students should receive many opportunities during which to connect literacy and active thought.

Reading theorist David Rumelhart describes the reading process as *interactive.* In other words, the reader acts on the text being read and the text works on the reader. Reader variables such as race, gender, age, socioeconomic status, and level of educational attainment affect the way in which the respective reader comprehends the text. Yet, the way in which the reader perceives letters, vocabulary, and syntax also affects the way in which the text is comprehended.

Readers read on two different levels, according to a foremost theorist in literary response, Louise Rosenblatt. Rosenblatt concludes that readers read from either one of two stances, the *aesthetic* or the *efferent.* Within the first stance, the reader is *experiencing* the literary work as a piece of art and *responding emotionally* to plot, setting, and characterization. With the efferent stance, the reader is engaged in the process of information-seeking. The reader engages with the text to primarily acquire information.

Children should have the opportunity to sharpen the skills needed for both aesthetic and efferent reading and eventually reach understanding that reading is interactive in nature. In relation to aesthetic readings, they should get chances to participate in reader response groups. In these small groups, they share their aesthetic experiences with books with other students. In reader response groups, students may generate questions about literature, make predictions, respond to the books read as well as to each other, and develop a greater appreciation of literary art.

Students should also be presented with chances to write about their reading. Through the use of reader response journals, students should be encouraged to jot down their thoughts and feelings about books and ideas.

They should also be exposed to other forms of text, such as those that are expository in nature (newspapers, magazines and informational books). Children should be taught to critically evaluate these forms. For instance, in reading allegedly factual accounts, how does one determine the author's credibility or bias? For what purpose and audience does the author write? How does one identify pivotal points? Are certain types of expository texts arranged in specific ways? Are there text patterns that can be deciphered?

Children should also receive the opportunity to write in expository fashion. They should be guided through the research process. For example, how does one generate research questions? What does the information-gathering process entail? How does one write in the most cogent manner possible and simultaneously convey information in a reader-friendly manner?

The research process may also present chances for students to learn more about computer technology and responsible use of it. For example, how does one "surf" the Internet? How does one determine the veracity of information received from it?

Students should additionally receive the understanding that the concept of literacy extends beyond the printed page. They should be provided chances to compare and contrast book and film versions of the same title in order to understand more comprehensively the similarities and differences between the two mediums. Further, they should understand that film is evaluated by different standards than are books, and books do not easily translate into film. Many decisions are made in the process of such translation.

In addition, they should receive the chance to evaluate art as a form of visual literacy and debate the value of television as an aspect of media literacy. Through the activities in which they are engaged, children should come to the realization that literacy defies simple definition.

INTERDISCIPLINARY TEACHING AND LEARNING

During the course of our days in the workplace, many of us use diversified skills and knowledge; our jobs require skills and knowledge of different content areas. For example, if one owns or operates a business, one relies on her knowledge of business concepts, mathematical ability, verbal skill, and understanding of interpersonal relations. The day is not compartmentalized so that these skills are used at specific points during the day. They are used as needed. Conversely, it seems odd that the school day is often compartmentalized according to subject matter.

Children, in many school settings, have reading at a certain point, social studies at another, and so on. More appropriately, children should be helped to see the connections between content areas. They should be led, through *interdisciplinary teaching and learning*, to the realization that the world is not a neat place and the knowledge required for survival is not isolated in various parts that are distinguishable as separate.

Students should be able to distinguish the ways in which historical periods affect the literary works, artistic and musical pieces, and scientific research produced. They should be able to understand the way in which changes in weather and climate (e.g., El Niño) have long-lasting effects on the way in which people live and their daily sustenance, as well as on the land, natural resources, and wild life.

Children should be encouraged to examine historical events from multiple perspectives and through multiple lenses, in an effort to reach the understanding that truth is relative and the world in which we live, ambiguous. For instance, World War II is perceived differently by U.S. soldiers who were Euro-American, those who were African American, the Japanese who were placed in internment camps here within the United States, the Japanese who experienced loss as a result of the U.S. decision to utilize the atomic bomb, those Europeans held and tortured in concentration camps, and world military powers. Each of these groups would be able to make legitimate points about the effects and consequences of war. Ultimately, however, the most important aspect of this discussion in a classroom would be the understanding that war has substantial human consequences for *all* involved.

Children should be presented with multiple sources (in the classroom) when attempting to make sense of such complex historical experiences rather than becoming reliant upon the "all-inclusive" and limited textbook. Through the use of multiple sources, children are led to become independent thinkers and view world events in the context of their true intricacy.

Unfortunately, the presentation of history and the world in a multifaceted manner causes as much angst as the inclusion of multicultural children's literature. As it stands, the approach to history presently utilized in most schools is either *contributions* or *additive*, according to leading multicultural education scholar James Banks, in his chapter entitled "Approaches to Multicultural Curriculum Reform." I frequently refer to the contributions approach as the minority-a-month plan. Banks characterizes it as studying other ethnicities and histories on special occasions, such as Martin Luther King, Jr.'s birthday, Black History month, or Native American month. In studying ethnic content in this manner, the message is easily conveyed that these groups are significant at certain times and insignificant much of the time.

The additive approach incorporates a few "token" books or facts about ethnic groups other than those categorized as European. Yet, largely, this approach serves as a means of appeasing so-called "special interest" groups without making substantive changes to the existing Eurocentric, mainstream curriculum. This method serves as a mere form of intellectual tokenism.

With these two approaches to curriculum integration, heroines and heroes for our children are chosen on the basis of passivity or their life histories are modified to make them assimilationist in nature. For instance, neither Martin Luther King, Jr. nor Malcolm X were passive figures. Both fought for the rights of Blacks, and MLK was a vehement defender of rights for the poor. In school curriculums, however, MLK is portrayed solely as a pacifist. He was not killed because of his pacifism. He was killed because of his revolutionary and radical thought on social change. Malcolm X should be remembered not only for his conversion but also for his uncompromising demand for social justice.

When presented with critical diversions from academic tradition and requests to transform the curriculum so that the history and perspectives of those from traditionally marginalized cultures are included in a tangible fashion, those in power (school administrators and boards of education) tend to fight strenuously to maintain the status quo. A prevailing thought seems to be that an interest in one's own history and culture might lead to hatred of the mainstream. I find this a false and ludicrous dichotomy. Children of all races and ethnicities can be led to understand that not all Whites are racist. Antiracist, White role models such as William Lloyd Garrison and Lucretia Coffin Mott should also be introduced and celebrated.

Another excuse used to maintain the status quo is that such inclusions serve as diversions from the curriculum. If this is the rationale used for maintaining inaccurate and incomplete versions of history, then the extant curriculum should not only be examined, it should be totally revamped.

In reiteration, your child deserves the best education possible. As such, it is your responsibility to ensure that your child receives assistance in the development of the critical literacy and thinking skills needed for political and economic empowerment in the 21st century. That development includes receiving a complete and accurate picture of her ethnic history and its relationship to the history of other ethnic and racial groups throughout the world.

CRITICAL LITERACY DEVELOPMENT IN THE HOME AND THE OLDER CHILD

Within your home, I anticipate that the effective literacy development practices that you have implemented are continuing. Yet, it might become more challenging to keep your child engaged with literacy as he grows older. It might also become more difficult to keep your youngster engaged with school.

Studies conducted by researcher Penny Oldfeather suggest that students routinely begin losing interest in school during grades four and five. For many teachers and teacher educators, the pivotal questions are: Why does this phenomenon occur? What changes from early elementary to the upper grades? It seems that research supports the observations that Black children, generally, have a much less positive experience in the upper elementary classroom than their White counterparts. For example, Black girls receive fewer positive feedback statements and fewer response opportunities in class. Black boys are more likely to be in the lowest academic track, and they are more likely to be judged inaccurately by teachers.

For parents and caregivers, the most salient questions might be: What can I do to prevent this loss of interest? How do I maintain my child's interest in both literacy and school? One of the first ways in which to ensure your child's continued interest might be to reinforce the importance of academic success, but also bring literacy off the printed page. You may wish to assist your child in making the connection between academic interests and fun.

READING, TALK, AND THE OLDER CHILD

When your child was younger, he frequently read the books you selected. As your child becomes older, however, he will develop his own interests. Talk to your child about those things that are of interest to him and reassure the child that his interests are self-generated rather than designed to please you. Help your child to make book selections based on interest. Encourage her to explore interests through the use of library books, as well as books, magazines, and newspapers that are purchased.

While it could potentially prove unenjoyable to read whole texts to older children, reading short excerpts from books, poems, and newspaper articles might be more palatable. If you run across a short piece that might be interesting or spark a dialogue, read it to your child. You might also choose to initiate or continue with the family book discussion groups suggested in Chapter 4.

Other ways to encourage the development of a critical reader include making literacy real and significant. Help your children use literacy to improve life for themselves and others. There will be many opportunities for the exploration of complex problems through literacy. For instance, if you and your child notice a problem within your community or society at large, use the chance to investigate the problem and attempt resolving it. This type of activism might include writing letters, responding to an inaccurate newspaper or television account, submitting op-ed pieces to local newspapers, researching the origin of respective problems, or initiating community discussion, protests, or projects. It might include the initiation of family projects as well. Assist your children in reaching the conclusion that literacy is a powerful tool and can be used for their benefit.

TELEVISION AND THE OLDER CHILD

It has already been addressed, within the context of this book, that television is a powerful and omnipresent force. Secondly, children are greatly attracted to the medium. Yet, whereas we previously discussed educational programming, this subsection centers on prime-time viewing.

For many parents, the primary issues that surround television programming seem to be the plausible effects that images of violence, explicit sex, and questionable language (so pervasive on television) might have on their children. Additionally, parents and caregivers resent the perceived irresponsibility of the media. But it is crucial that parents understand one key point about television.

Television programming, in all of its varied forms, is designed to generate profit. Its content is shaped to attract advertisers, and the more controversy surrounding a show, the better. Advertisers see the proposition in the following manner: More viewers means more potential customers. Humanitarian concerns, including the potential harm or influence on the minds of the young, have been and remain of secondary importance. So, what is a parent to do?

For some parents, the answer might lie in forbidding children to view television shows that are considered controversial. With young children, forbidding might prove effective. With older children, however, the fact that you forbid television or controversial programming in your home does not decrease the likelihood that your children will be exposed to it. If everyone is talking about it, rest assured that your child (in most instances) will not wish to be excluded. A friend with older children would forbid them to watch television when she was not at home. She would run her hand across the top of the television (for heat) when she returned. Although she claims this method worked for her, most parents find that their children simply become adept at deception and turn the television off in time for it to sufficiently cool.

It might prove more beneficial to concentrate on teaching older children ways in which to become critical consumers of television rather than be taken in by its ploys. Teach your child to operate from a position of strength as opposed to one of passivity.

Determine, with your child, an appropriate number of viewing hours. Many parents believe that guidelines should be set between two and ten hours a week. It is best to consider input from your child. It may also prove helpful for you both to monitor the way in which your child uses her or his time for a week. Pinpoint times during which television could be watched without interfering with other responsibilities such as homework, household chores, and other things. You might also consider whether the viewing of videotapes should be included in the allotted number of viewing hours.

Help your child to make informed choices about television programming. Assist your child in reading the television guide each week and completing a viewing chart. In this way, your child's choices are clearly established. Thus, the allotted times are posted and your child's viewing time is reserved.

Be consistent. Once a specific number of viewing hours has been determined and agreed on, help your child abide by those guidelines. Do not waiver or indiscriminately add viewing hours.

It might also be advisable to encourage children to view the evening news intermittently. Discuss with them the ways in which news programs are designed (e.g., top news stories appear first, then those of local interest, national, international, weather, sports, and feature). Discuss the ways in which people of color and the communities in which we live are portrayed, as well as ways in which news is filtered and shaped to take on the values of the mainstream.

When a controversial viewing choice arises, discuss it with your child before the actual airing. Voice your concerns and afford your child the opportunity to share her or his reasons for watching the show. Then, agree to watch the program with your child. Afterward, spend time discussing the images presented and their potential impact. Ask your child questions about her or his perception of what was seen, as well as about the value of particular views expressed on the show. Subsequently, if you would prefer that your child opt against further viewing of the show, voice that concern.

While parents and caregivers cannot totally ward off the harmful influences of television, I believe that they are able to enhance their children's ability to make choices and expose children to their thoughts and feelings about television programming. In this way, they are opening the doors to dialogue with their children, in addition to establishing themselves as fair and open-minded; these are qualities that most of us desire that our children emulate.

In relation to media, a word of caution should also be provided about the Internet. Just as parents should monitor their children's use of television, they should also monitor the children's surfing of the "Net." At this point, the Internet remains unregulated. There is no control over those who use the Internet to either transmit or receive information. You, as a parent and caregiver, must be vigilant. We have seen a frightening use of the Net in numerous cases in which teens used extreme violence.

HOMEWORK

One dilemma that parents and upper elementary grade children frequently mention during our conversations is homework. As your child progresses through the upper grades, homework should increase in volume and difficulty. Your child should have homework most days of the school week. If there is a lack of clarity on daily homework requirements, contact the school's administrative offices or the school's district office and request a copy of the state guidelines concerning homework. Those guidelines should clearly explain existing policies on homework, including whether homework should be assigned daily, the amount of time allotted (daily) for homework, and so forth.

It might also prove helpful to ask for a copy of the academic standards required for successful completion of the grade in which your child is currently placed. In this way, you will gain some sense of the content that is supposed to be addressed in your child's respective class. However, it does not prove beneficial to interrogate your child's teacher about minor points that are not being addressed in respect to subject matter. It is essential that you bring your concern to the teacher if you believe that major curricular concepts are being neglected.

It would, probably, prove helpful if you established household guidelines for homework completion, as well. You might wish to consider questions such as: Where should homework assignments be completed? At what time should they be done? Should I check homework before it is placed in bookbags for submission the next day? You might also consider the issue of distractions. Do the television, radio, and calls from friends distract my child from focusing on her or his homework? Also, once homework procedures are in place, remain consistent with your child regarding them. If homework is to be completed after dinner, remain firm on that policy. If television is not allowed during homework completion, do not concede on the issue simply because your child expresses displeasure. Remember these rules are in place as a means of ensuring your child's academic success. Concomitantly, you are sending the message that academic achievement is important in your home.

Review your child's notebook and completed homework assignments routinely. Check to ensure that class notes are being taken every day and homework is assigned. Look for the dates of class notes and homework assignments and examine content. In fact, provide your child with a special notebook or portion of her or his notebook to be used exclusively for writing down homework assignments.

In respect to assisting your child with homework, it is essential that you understand the purpose of homework. Homework should be a *reinforcement* of classwork. Homework helps your child practice the skill learned or gain a more comprehensive understanding of the concept addressed that day. Homework should not be used as an opportunity to introduce new concepts or skills. When asking for your assistance, your child should be able to clearly explain the information learned and that should assist you in helping your child with homework. If you find that either you or your child is too frequently unclear about homework requirements, you should make an effort to contact her or his teacher for clarification.

Studies suggest, regardless of socioeconomic status, parents greatly enhance the success of their youngsters by taking their roles as home instructors seriously.

Chapter 9

Of Special Concern— Reading Disability

Words are the way to know ecstasy. Without them life is barren.
—bell hooks, Black Feminist Scholar
(*Wounds of Passion: A Writing Life*)

Although African Americans generally hold great respect for education, they are suspect of school systems. The educational experiences of Blacks in many school systems, nationwide, indicate that the suspicion is justified and warranted.

Standardized testing (both achievement and intelligence quotient tests) have, historically, been used to stigmatize Blacks and validate unfair claims of Black intellectual inferiority. Incommensurate numbers of Black children are academically underprepared, tracked, suspended, retained, expelled, and have school disciplinary action taken against them in U.S. schools. Additionally, Black youngsters are disproportionately placed in special education programs geared toward children with learning disabilities and emotional disturbances. Yet, they remain underrepresented in classes for the gifted and talented.

Feelings of distrust toward school systems are compounded for parents and caregivers of Black children with special needs. For many of these families, school personnel and administrations are adversarial in the process of "helping," especially when diagnoses and classifications are questioned. Although there are many teachers and administrators who take their responsibilities seriously and fervently desire to assist the children in their charge, school is a system and often fails to deal effectively with children who exhibit difficulties in conforming to the norm. In many such instances, it is the advocacy of parents and caregivers that makes the difference and ensures respectful and compassionate handling of such children within schools.

Hopefully, this chapter will assist families in negotiating complex and bureaucratic school systems as they seek to help their children when a plausible reading disability is brought to their attention.

I would be professionally remiss, however, if I failed to mention the following point. The first step for families (when confronted by teachers or school administrations with a child's possible reading disability) is to schedule a comprehensive physical examination for the child with your family physician. This course of action serves to determine that there is no physical cause for the problem, for example, sight or hearing loss or neurological impairment.

WHAT IS READING DISABILITY?

Current figures suggest that the majority of special needs children are categorized as having speech or communication disorders. Recent figures indicate that the percentage of special needs children diagnosed with such disorders hovers near 50%. Most of those classified as having difficulties with speech and communication are in the early elementary grades. Although it has been estimated that approximately 60% of six-year-olds require assistance with speech difficulties, only 5% of 11–year-old students need these services.

Calculations suggest that more than 40% of kindergarten students and 25% of first-graders have minor speech impediments. The disorders include reversals, inability to sound out certain combinations and respective speech sounds, mispronunciations, and departures in pitch and loudness. Some of these noted difficulties are affected by race and class. Thus, there are times during which differences (attributable to dialect or second-language acquisition), compounded by school professionals' lack of familiarity with and knowledge of specific cultural dynamics, might be identified as speech deficits.

Speech difficulties manifest themselves in a multitude of forms. Yet, they are most commonly grouped according to four categories: articulatory (an inability to produce certain sounds or sound combinations), voice (pitch or volume), linguistic (inclusive of language delay), and rhythmic problems (e.g., stuttering).

Although speech and communication disorders are identified as the most common special-needs classification, the fastest growing categorizations are reading and learning disabilities. The link between reading and learning disabilities is made because reading disabilities are subsumed under learning disabilities in most of the professional literature. Further, the two terms are often used synonymously in educational practice.

Reading disability is a perplexing term to define. First of all, there is not a significant way in which to distinguish reading disability from poor reading skill, with the exception of a diagnosed biological impairment that hinders the reading process. Otherwise, the diagnosis of reading disability (that can be inclusive of word processing and phonological difficulties) is largely a subjective determination.

In their book *Off Track: When Poor Readers Become "Learning Disabled,"* authors Louise Spear-Swerling and Robert Sternberg state that federal legislation guidelines for the classification of reading disability are ambiguous and open to interpretation from state to state. There are other subjective distinctions made within states, on a district by district basis. Thus, a child who is considered to have a reading-disability in one state might not be so diagnosed in another, or a child classified as reading-disabled in one school district of a state might be miraculously "cured" simply by moving and attending school in another district.

Additionally, most special-needs referrals and placements have little to do with a child's inherent aptitudes. Many such decisions are based on external variables such as race, gender, socioeconomic status, and classroom behavior. Therefore a poor, Black male child, who exhibits difficulty in reading and whom the teacher perceives as lacking self-control in the classroom, is much more likely to be identified as reading or learning disabled than a White female student (with the same difficulty reading but whom the teacher perceives as well-behaved and quiet in the classroom). This practice proves inherently unfair to both children.

Another point that can be made about the nebulous nature of reading disability is that there is no way to truly distinguish a student who is actually disabled from a student whose learning style and preferences are not being tapped within a classroom or who is receiving ineffective instruction. In a number of instances, it is easier for the teacher to identify a student as learning-disabled than to reexamine the efficacy of her or his teaching style, expectations of students, and instructional methods.

Once a diagnosis of reading disability has been made, there are problems as well. Although I have encountered some students who have described their diagnoses of learning disabled as a godsend because they no longer felt "stupid," many others have been hindered by the identification. They have been stigmatized by the label, made to feel that their chances for academic progress were nonexistent, and developed a "learned helplessness" that prevented them from even attempting academic tasks that were within their grasp of understanding. For many of these students, envisioning the mere possibility of attending college proved an impossibility.

As can be gleaned from the preceding pages of this chapter, the process of special education identification and classification should be approached with great caution. With these diagnoses and treatments, there are long-lasting implications for your child and your family that should be thoughtfully considered.

Yet, what is a parent or caregiver to do when faced with a teacher's or school administrator's conjecture that her or his child is reading or learning disabled?

WHAT IS IN THE BEST INTEREST OF MY CHILD?

Although such a situation is rife with anxiety, frustration, and can be intimidating, parents and caregivers' first responsibility is to remain mindful that they are their children's most ardent educational advocates. They, more so than others, should be aware of their children's strengths and weaknesses. *Do not anxiously accept the labels that others give your children.*

Approach the predicament with time and care. Ultimately, you must be *certain* that your child is in need of special education. The decision is not one that can be revoked easily. It is frequently much more difficult to exit special education services than it is to enter. After taking your child for a complete medical examination, the next step is to confer with the teacher about the conjecture. Upon which criteria is the determination based? Is it possible that the judgment is a premature one?

In justification of the conjecture, some teachers will mention that a child has difficulty completing assignments in a timely fashion, "doesn't seem to understand what's going on," seems to have difficulty reading passages aloud, or consistently reverses letters in reading and writing. In some instances, behavioral problems the child is perceived to experience will also be broached as a means of establishing distractibility or perceived embarrassment about academic difficulties. In a case such as the one described, the parent or caregiver should remain vigilant in determining whether the teacher appears to be basing the conjecture solely on observable classroom behaviors or assumptions and beliefs. After all, this book has broached the topic of teacher expectation and the manner in which teacher beliefs about students often lead to self-fulfilling prophecies, in which students actually behave in a manner that confirms the projections made about them. If the teacher is vague and general about the student behaviors that led to the determination that there could be learning deficits, ask for specific incidents and clarification.

It is also important to examine the teacher's perception within the context that it is made. It becomes necessary to distinguish whether the teacher's determination seems reflective of an understanding of children's capabilities (as per age and developmental level), as well as the cognitive processing associated with literacy development. For example, a child in grades K through 2 might appropriately exhibit distractibility and letter reversal, as per the level of her literacy development, exposure to books, and classroom instruction. The behaviors might be symptomatic of a child struggling to make sense of literacy or who would benefit from different instructional methods and pedagogical techniques. Nothing described could be immediately construed as "abnormal" for a youngster in the early elementary grades.

Conversely, there might be cause for concern if an older child (in grades 3 through 6) is exhibiting an inability to complete class assignments, read passages aloud, and reverses letters in reading and writing. Yet, in this scenario as well, it remains difficult to determine whether the child is truly having difficulty grasping literacy concepts or his learning needs remain unmet.

It might be possible that the child is experiencing a personal crisis (e.g., divorce, the death of a parent, attending a new school, interpersonal difficulties with classmates) that has affected academic progress and of which the teacher is unaware. In such an instance, conferencing with the parent or caregiver might yield this information and assist the teacher in better serving the child during this troublesome time.

It is also possible that the youngster is being taught with methods and materials that do not make sense to her or have been determined a waste of time. Therefore, it is important to speak to your child about his perceptions of academic progress made, teachers, and classroom atmosphere. It would also prove beneficial, during the course of your conference with the teacher, to ascertain (in a nonconfrontational manner) whether the teacher has received any additional training in diagnosing reading disability. It remains your right to know the qualifications of the person assessing your child's alleged disability and to determine for yourself whether the observations presented are consistent with those you have made in your home.

Teachers might also base their conjectures regarding a perceived reading disability on an "observable" discrepancy between IQ and achievement. In other words, the child seems to be of average or above-average intelligence, yet has difficulty in reading. In this scenario, the student should excel in other academic subject areas while a distinct deficit may be observed in literacy development or spelling. Once again, the diagnosis is not clear-cut.

First of all, the teacher has no truly accurate means of determining a child's intelligence. Thus, the determination is based on subjective measures (e.g., observation, teacher-generated tests, and conclusions reached about the student's home and prior educational experiences). Such measures are open to interpretation. Even if the teacher were privy to both a child's IQ and standardized achievement test scores and based the determination of reading disability on those respective scores, his diagnosis would remain problematic.

As determined previously, standardized testing has proved unfair to Blacks historically. In many districts nationwide, it is illegal to use culturally and linguistically biased measures (e.g., IQ tests), as a sole means of making special education evaluations. Further, in reference to IQ tests, such tests are designed under the premise that IQ is static; in other words, your intelligence seems to remain the same throughout your life and indicates whether you should be perceived as "smart" or "dumb." I find this mode of viewing intelligence questionable and prefer to view it as a fluid process instead.

For these reasons, I find Howard Gardner's *Frames of Mind: The Theory of Multiple Intelligences* much more palatable. According to Gardner, there are seven types of intelligence; this model departs from the traditional model that bases intelligence on linguistic and logical-mathematical knowledge and ability. The multiple intelligences include linguistic, logical-mathematical, spatial (ability to draw and design), musical, kinesthetic (ability to use body like athletes and dancers), interpersonal (getting along with others), and intrapersonal (knowing one's self). This model is also based on the premise that people exhibit intelligence in two or three of these domains. Therefore, a person may be gifted in several respective areas.

If the teacher uses your child's standardized test scores as a basis of an identification regarding a reading disability, ask if there are other authentic measures that have been used to confirm the test score results. For example, if the teacher mentions her or his classroom observations of the child, ask if anecdotal records have been maintained and if they might be shared with you. Anecdotal records are documented (written) notes, kept by the teacher, that describe children's classroom progress. You might also ask if portfolios are maintained. If they are, you might ask to see samples of your child's work taken from her or his portfolio that might support the teacher's observations and concerns.

Once the teacher has presented her conjectures, you might wish to ask her advice on the manner in which you should proceed (as an advocate for your child). Teachers might suggest ways in which you might assist your child at home, that you consider obtaining tutorial services for the child, or that you give permission for school-based testing for reading disability and the initiation of the special education process.

If you find that the existence of a reading disability has not been fully substantiated, then you should share your perception with the teacher and work toward some agreement in which you both incorporate additional measures to assist your child in making progress, in respect to literacy development. You might also wish to reassure the teacher that you are grateful for her or his concern and will continue to consider the observations presented. However, at this particular point, you would like to give your child every opportunity to succeed without the stigma of special education labels.

Conversely, if you decide that it would be best to initiate the process of special education identification and testing, learn as much as you can about the process and follow it very carefully. Be an active participant in the hope of securing all the assistance you can for your child.

WHAT STEPS MIGHT BE TAKEN IN THE HOME TO ASSIST A CHILD BELIEVED TO HAVE A READING DISABILITY?

If you have decided to postpone or forego the process of special education testing and identification, you should maintain close contact with school personnel (especially your child's teacher). You might opt to spend time observing or volunteering in your child's classroom. Confer with your child's teacher on a routine basis to closely monitor your child's literacy development and academic progress. Ask questions about methods used. For instance, if you observe that the teacher seems to focus almost exclusively on meaning-emphasized approaches to reading, ask about the inclusion of strategies that are code-based. If you find that the teacher is unable or unwilling to vary strategies, investigate professional tutoring possibilities or a class change.

Further, read as much of the professional literature as you can find on helping children who have poor reading skills. In this way, you will approach your child's reading challenges strategically and knowledgeably.

Appendix A: Suggested Books

I understood education before I understood anything else. From the time I was two, my mother said "You will go to college. Education is the key to survival" and I understood that.
—Melba Patillo Beals, Activist and one of the nine children to desegregate Central High School in Little Rock, Arkansas in 1957 (as quoted in Tamara Nikuradse's *My Mother had a Dream: African-American Women Share Their Mothers' Words of Wisdom*)

BOARD BOOKS

Baby's Bedtime
Author: Nikki Grimes
Illustrator: Sylvia Walker
Publication Date: 1995
Price: $3.95

As Baby nears bedtime, Mom and Dad happily share the responsibilities of preparing him for bed. Mom bathes and dresses Baby. Dad reads a bedtime story and sings a lullaby. The rhyming text and warm illustrations make this book a bedtime favorite for young children.

Baby's Colors
Author: Naomi McMillan
Illustrator: Keaf Holliday
Publication Date: 1995
Price: $3.95

In *Baby's Colors*, a young toddler dressed in a particular color for the day also interacts with a familiar doll, toy, blanket, or stuffed animal of the same color. Preschoolers will love learning or reinforcing their colors as each sturdy page is turned.

Reproduced courtesy of Essence Books for Children.

Brown Bear, Brown Bear, What Do You See?
Author: Bill Martin Jr.
Illustrator: Eric Carle
Publication Date: 1995, 1970, 1967
Price: $6.95 (paper)

Young children love the repetition, as different animals are asked to describe what they see. Through this book, toddlers and preschoolers become acquainted with the concepts of both animals and colors.

Chicka Chicka ABC
Author: Bill Martin Jr. and John Archambault
Illustrator: Lois Ehlert
Publication Date: 1993, 1989
Price: $4.95 (paper)

In this rhythmic, frollicking tale, each letter of the alphabet tries to makes its way up a coconut tree. *Chicka Chicka ABC* is a story that young children seem to love hearing again and again. It is a personal favorite of this reader's daughter.

I Can Count
Author: Denise Lewis Patrick
Illustrator: Fred Willingham

Publication Date: 1996
Price: $3.99 (paper)

This book is an excellent one for toddlers and preschoolers. It will familiarize and encourage them to count from one to ten, in addition to seeing number words in context. The illustrations show a young Black boy counting with toys, maracas, books, sailboats, musical instruments, puppies, puppets, blocks, cars, and animals.

Let's Go to the Petting Zoo with Jungle Jack
Author: Jack Hanna/Lucy Herring
Illustrator: Neil Brennan
Publication Date: 1992
Price: $10.00 (paper)

Exotic zoo animals and the textures of their body coverings are introduced to young readers in this interactive book. As they flip the pages, children are encouraged to feel the llama's fur and touch the penguin chick's down. Many readers will return to this book again and again.

Miss Spider's Tea Party: The Counting Book
Author/Illustrator: David Kirk
Publication Date: 1997
Price: $8.95 (paper)

Through this vividly colored, brilliantly illustrated book, young children are introduced to Miss Spider as she attempts to hold a tea party. There's just one problem . . . the potential guests are afraid of her. The concepts of numbers (1 to 12) and insects are also reinforced in this selection.

My Daddy and I
Author: Eloise Greenfield
Illustrator: Jan Spivey Gilchrist
Publication Date: 1991
Price: $5.95 (paper)

In this lively book, a young boy and his dad spend time together. They paint, do laundry, and play ball, among other things. This reader found it endearing that the duo engaged in both activities typically perceived to be for females as well as those perceived to be male-oriented.

No Diapers for Baby
Author: Denise Lewis Patrick
Illustrator: Sylvia Walker
Publication Date: 1995
Price: $3.95

Baby wants to be a big girl. No more diapers for her! An accessible story line and inviting illustrations help parents introduce the topic of potty training to their young toddlers. The book's sturdy construction, however, enables toddlers to view the book on their own, again and again.

Peekaboo, Baby
Author: Denise Lewis Patrick
Illustrator: Ray Simmons
Publication Date: 1995
Price: $3.95

Playing peekaboo is a favorite of the baby presented in this book. The bright, vivid illustrations bring this lively story to life.

The Very Hungry Caterpillar
Author/Illustrator: Eric Carle
Publication Date: 1987, 1969
Price: $9.95

The very hungry caterpillar eats his way to metamorphosis in this selection. Through the use of bright illustrations and interactive book design, Carle introduces the days of the week, counting, and transformation.

POETRY

Brown Honey in Broomwheat Tea
Author: Joyce Carol Thomas
Illustrator: Floyd Cooper
Publication Date: 1993
Price: $5.95

This book features a beautiful collection of poems about family, individuality, and pride of heritage. Told from a young girl's perspective, the narrator admonishes us to love ourselves and be proud of who we are. She is young, spirited, and happy! The poems discuss her mother, father, and sister, as well as the vicissitudes of life and the careful choice of the place one occupies in the world. Floyd Cooper's paintings will also capture the hearts of readers.

The Dreamkeepers and Other Poems
Author: Langston Hughes
Illustrator: Brian Pinkney
Publication Date: 1994
Price: $7.99

In this brilliant collection of poems that is accompanied by the dazzling artwork of Brian Pinkney, young readers are introduced to the premier Black poet Langston Hughes. Young people get to share a poetry that embodies "hope, dreams, aspiration, love and life . . . poems about his people, for his people, poems for each and everyone of us," states poet Lee Bennett Hopkins.

From a Child's Heart
Author: Nikki Grimes
Illustrator: Brenda Joysmith
Publication Date: 1993
Price: $15.95 (hardcover); $7.95 (paper)

This exceptional collection of Christian prayer poems is written from the perspective of children. The poems masterfully reflect children's hopes, dreams, fears, desires, and attempts to make sense of a complex and ever-changing world.

Harlem: A Poem
Author: Walter Dean Myers
Illustrator: Christopher Myers
Publication Date: 1997
Price: $16.95 (hardcover)

Through this Caldecott Honor Book, Walter Dean Myers and his son, Christopher, celebrate Harlem with words and illustrations. The vibrancy of the pictures brings the poem to life. While reading, the reader can feel a distinctive, rhythmic beat. The poem brings us the story of those who migrated to New York City and established a Mecca we can all call home. Myers shares the notability of a region that has inspired such greats as Countee Cullen, James Baldwin, and Malcolm X. As readers, we can feel the rhythm, share in the fun, witness everyday happenings, and feel the pain of a place that has touched so many.

Honey, I Love and Other Poems
Author: Eloise Greenfield
Illustrators: Leo and Diane Dillon
Publication Date: 1978
Price: $4.95 (paper)

The voice represented in these poems is simple and serene. Young readers are able to obtain glimpses of the young narrator's cherished life. The poems reflect joy, happiness, and peace. The illustrations, done in black and white, only serve to enhance the pleasure experienced after reading. All children will be able to reflect on some aspect brought to life through these verses.

In Daddy's Arms I Am Tall: African Americans Celebrating Fathers
Illustrator: Javaka Steptoe
Publication Date: 1997
Price: $15.95 (hardcover)

The poems that are included in this volume focus on the special relationship shared between children and their fathers. Although the poets come from many different walks of life, they share two significant bonds of commonality: warm memories and thoughts of their fathers and grandfathers, in addition to pride in their African American heritage. In tribute to his father, John, Javaka Steptoe uses a multimedia approach in the stunning illustrations that fill the pages of this book.

Lift Every Voice and Sing
Author: James Weldon Johnson
Illustrator: Jan Spivey Gilchrist
Publication Date: 1995
Price: $14.95

The lyrics to the Black national anthem are given visual representation in this inspirational picture storybook. Past, present, and future merge with each stunning illustration.

My Black Me: A Beginning Book of Black Poetry
Editor: Arnold Adoff
Publication dates: 1994, 1974
Price: $14.00 (hardcover); $4.99 (paper)

This compilation of poems concomitantly focuses on the beauty of being Black and introduces young readers to some of the most noted Black poets (e.g., Langston Hughes, Nikki Giovanni and Amiri Baraka among others). The poetry, inspirational and powerful, is warm and inviting to children and adults alike.

Night on Neighborhood Street
Author: Eloise Greenfield
Illustrator: Spiven Gilchrist
Publication Date: 1991
Price: $5.99 (paper)

A lyrical collection, this set of poems brings together the concepts of family, neighborhood, and community. There are poems about bedtime, church gatherings, childhood sleepovers, and unemployment. Both sadness and joy are expressed, but the overall theme of family unity shines through. The aptly drawn, pastel-colored illustrations add to this collection's beauty as well.

Shake It to the One that You Love the Best: Play Songs and Lullabies from Black Musical Traditions
Editor: Cheryl Warren Mattox
Illustrators: Varnette P. Honeywood and Brenda Joysmith
Publication Date: 1991
Price: $9.95 (paper and audiocassette)

These notable play songs and lullabies serve as a terrific way with which to reacquaint yourself and introduce your children to forgotten songs of youth. The book and audiocassette provide us with a way in which to share a piece of the past and continue a significant component of the collective Black oral tradition.

PICTURE STORYBOOKS

Abuela
Author/Illustrator: Arthur Dorros

Publication Date: 1991
Price: $14.00 (hardcover)

While riding the bus with her grandmother Abuela, Rosalba imagines that they are soaring over the sights of New York City. The marvelous collage illustrations allowed this reader to travel with Rosalba and her Abuela through the bustling streets, pigeon-filled parks, and storefronts of the city. The diverse groups of people also leaped from the page, capturing the true essence of New York City. The use of Spanish phrases, with English, helped to convey the duality of Rosalba's rich heritage as both a Latino and American.

Aida
Author: Leontyne Price
Illustrators: Leo and Dianne Dillon
Publication Date: 1990
Price: $16.95

Opera singer Leontyne Price lends a skillful hand to this retelling of Verdi's opera of the same name. Ethiopian princess, Aida, falls in love with Radames, an Egyptian general. Yet, the love shared between the two ultimately ends in tragedy. The colorful, glossy pages of this picture storybook superbly depict the honor, beauty, courage, and emotion of its central characters.

Amazing Grace
Author: Mary Hoffman
Illustrator: Caroline Binch
Publication Date: 1991
Price: $13.95

Grace, a young girl who loves stories and imaginative play, wants to play the lead in the school play, *Peter Pan*. Yet, Grace's schoolmates tell her that she can't because she is Black and a girl. Ultimately, Grace comes to realize that she can do anything she sets her mind to. Hoffman has created a strong and confident character in Grace, who does not allow society to define her identity or her dreams. She believes in herself and she is encouraged by a supportive family.

Ashanti to Zulu: African Traditions
Author: Margaret Musgrove

Illustrators: Leo and Diane Dillon
Publication Date: 1976
Price: $4.99

In this collection of vignettes, 26 African tribes are alphabetically introduced to young readers. The vignettes all reflect African tribal customs, traditions, or values. A great book from which to learn about African heritage, the collection focuses on the vastness of Africa and the diversity of its people. The outstanding artwork was completed in warm earth tones and splendid detail.

Aunt Flossie's Hats (and Crab Cakes Later)
Author: Elizabeth Fitzgerald Howard
Illustrator: James Ransome
Publication Date: 1991
Price: $14.95 (hardcover)

Sarah and Susan love to visit their great-great-Aunt Flossie on Sunday afternoons. Those are the times during which each unique hat of Aunt Flossie's that the girls try on reminds her of a time past. The elder and younger generations enjoy time together through the sharing of tea, cookies, crab cakes, and stories. The illustrations in this book, oil paintings, were outstanding.

Baseball Saved Us
Author: Ken Mochizuki
Illustrator: Dom Lee
Publication Date: 1993
Price: $6.95

A Japanese American boy learns to play baseball during the time in which he and his family are forced to live in a U.S. internment camp during World War II. While his newly acquired skill helps him when the war is over, the other lessons he learns about racism, relocation, prejudice, and the significance of identity remain with him a lifetime.

Bible Stories from the Old Testament in Three Dimensions
Author: C. Kondeatis
Publication Date: 1991
Price: $17.95

This pop-up book features five stories from the Old Testament. They include: the Garden of Eden, David and Goliath, Noah, the Tower of Babel, and the parting of the Red Sea. All are explored in three-dimensional scenes. This reader loved the book. The pop-up illustrations added to the power of the Bible's words in a manner that would not otherwise have been possible. While opening the pages, the reader can actually envision the Red Sea dividing as Moses extends his hands before it or see the enormous size of Noah's ark.

The Bracelet
Author: Yoshiko Uchida
Illustrator: Joanna Yardley
Publication Data: 1996, 1993
Price: $14.95 (hardcover); $5.95 (paper)

A young Japanese American girl, Emi, and her family are interned in a prison camp during World War II. As a result of being forced from her home, Emi feels displaced and homesick. Her one saving grace appears to be a bracelet, given to her by her friend Laurie as a keepsake and reminder of their friendship. Emi receives another gift, much more significant than the bracelet, with its loss.

Bright Eyes, Brown Skin
Authors: Cheryl Willis Hudson
and Bernette G. Ford
Illustrator: George Ford
Publication Date: 1990
Price: $6.95

Olivia, Jordan, Alexa, and Ethan are bright, spirited children who enjoy their days at school. Preschoolers will be able to enjoy the rhythmic text and easily identify with the playful, cooperative children presented in the story.

Brown Angels
Author: Walter Dean Myers
Publication Date: 1993
Price: $5.95 (paper)

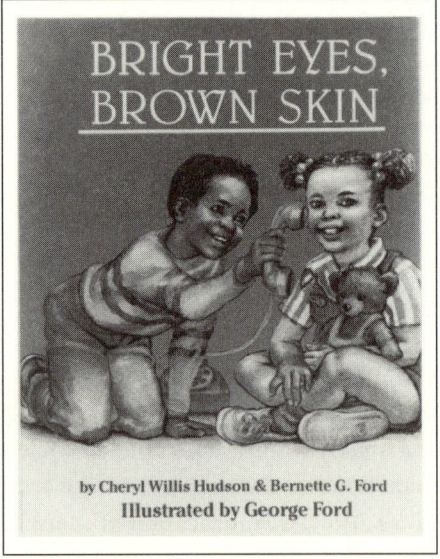

by Cheryl Willis Hudson & Bernette G. Ford
Illustrated by George Ford

Reproduced courtesy of Just Us Books.

In a compilation of eloquent poems and expressive, antique photographs, Myers presents a loving portrait of Black children. The photographs revealed the innocence, delight, hardship, and hope of the children they introduce to readers.

Buffalo Dance
Author: Nancy Van Loan
Illustrator: Beatriz Vidal
Publication Date: 1993
Price: $15.95

Buffalo Dance, a potent Native American legend, is the story of a woman's courage, the way in which she saves her village and brings about the ritual of the Buffalo Dance. Through the dance, the Blackfoot tribe showed their respect to the buffalo for sacrificing their own so that the tribe could survive. Blackfoot patterns and designs border each page. The magnificent illustrations aptly display the grand beauty of the Great Plains and a people who love the earth and all of its creatures.

A Chair for My Mother
Author and Illustrator: Vera B. Williams
Publication Date: 1982
Price: $15.00 (hardcover)

Through good times and bad, a child's bond with her mother and grandmother is maintained and strengthened. The wonderful illustrations of this story provided its most distinguishing feature. Each page was filled with bright hues, such as chartreuse, teal, and aqua, that brought an exuberant aura to the text. Additionally, the borders surrounding the varied illustrations told the story as aptly as did the text.

Chicken Sunday
Author/Illustrator: Patricia Polacco
Publication Date: 1992
Price: $15.95

Following church each Sunday morning, Miss Eula Mae, her grandsons Stewart and Winston, and their special neighbor and adopted sister always enjoy a delicious chicken dinner together. In appreciation of those special times provided by Miss Eula, the children decide to sell decorated eggs in an effort to buy her a hat she has longed for. In the process, the children are accused of a wrongful act in their neighborhood and must prove their innocence. The concepts of familial love, devotion, acceptance, and the worth of one's reputation are particularly noteworthy in this story.

Cinder-Elly
Author: Frances Minters
Illustrator: G. Brian Karas
Publication Date: 1994
Price: $13.99 (hardcover)

In this urban, upbeat variation of Cinder-Ella, the story is told in rap. Cinder-Elly lives in New York City, attends a basketball game instead of a ball, falls in love with a basketball player, and loses a slipper. Many children enjoy the contemporary nature of this version and get a kick out of trying to say the rap aloud without running out of breath.

Cornrows
Author: Camille Yarbrough
Illustrator: Carole Byard
Publication Date: 1979
Price: $5.99 (paper)

Great Grammaw shares history with her family as they inquire about the artistry involved in her hair cornrowing. She lovingly recounts her own memories, as well as those of her ancestors, and simultaneously elucidates the history of braids. This story reflects the pride and beauty of Black people. The illustrations, completed in black and white, present soft, fluid, and loving representations of Blackness.

The Day Gogo Went to Vote:
*   South Africa, 1994*
Author: Elinor Batezat Sisula
Illustrator: Sharon Wilson
Publication Date: 1996
Price: $14.95 (hardcover)

This wonderful story is told from the perspective of a young girl living in Soweto at the time of its first democratic election. Thembi becomes an active participant in her great-grandmother's first voting experience. This is a story of frustrations, struggle, joy, and ultimately respect. Through this

Reproduced courtesy of Little, Brown and Company.

picture storybook, the reader simultaneously shares in South Africa's contemporary history and experiences the warm, intergenerational ties shared between child and great-grandparent.

Dinner at Aunt Connie's House
Author/Illustrator: Faith Ringgold
Publication Date: 1993
Price: $4.95 (paper)

Melody is anticipating her annual family gathering at Aunt Connie's beach house. Each summer is filled with surprise. This summer, one of the surprises is a set of 12 beautiful portraits of famous Black women, painted by Aunt Connie (an artist). Melody and her cousin stumble on these paintings and, to their amazement, the portraits can speak.

Dumpling Soup
Author: Kim J. Rattigan
Publication Date: 1993
Price: $15.95

Young Marisa tries to carry out the family tradition of making New Year's Eve dumplings. Yet, she is afraid that her dumplings will not hold up to those of her grandmother, a veteran dumpling-maker. One of the most enjoyable features of this book was its focus on mixed heritage. Although the book is set in Hawaii, it embraces the diversity of Marisa's family. Various foods, languages, and customs tie Marisa's family together.

An Enchanted Hair Tale
Author: Alexis DeVeaux
Illustrator: Cheryl Hanna
Publication Date: 1987
Price: $4.95

Young Sudan has dreadlocks just like his mother. He loves that his hair is both wild and enchanted. Unfortunately, many grown-ups and children just don't understand. Sudan decides to go to an enchanted place where everyone does appreciate the beauty of his locked hair.

Encounter
Author: Jane Yolen
Illustrator: David Shannon
Publication Date: 1992
Price: $14.95 (hardcover)

In this stirring and powerful tale, a young inhabitant of the Americas warns his elders about the harm that will potentially come from Columbus's arrival on their land. They fail to listen and are faced with grave consequences. Although the words used by Yolen are carefully selected and the descriptions vivid, Shannon's illustrations add greatly to the story with their haunting beauty.

The Egyptian Cinderella
Author: Shirley Climo
Illustrator: Ruth Heller
Publication Date: 1989
Price: $15.00

In this rather clever spin on the traditional Cinderella tale, Climo tells the story of Rhodopis, a Greek maiden, enslaved in Egypt and discriminated against because of her blonde hair, green eyes, and fair complexion. One day, while doing chores, a falcon snatches her red slipper and delivers it to Amasis, the Pharoah. He takes the delivery as a sign that he should marry and sets out to find the owner of the slipper.

Everett Anderson's Goodbye
Author: Lucille Clifton
Illustrator: Ann Grifalconi
Publication Date: 1983
Price: $5.95 (paper)

Everett Anderson's father has died. Daddy is no longer there to go to the park or sit in his favorite chair. But Everett learns that death doesn't stop love. In this simple, yet complex, book, Clifton eloquently introduces young children to the concept of grief and the five stages of grieving as identified by Elizabeth Kubler-Ross.

Everett Anderson's Nine Month Long
Author: Lucille Clifton
Illustrator: Ann Grifalconi
Publication Date: 1978
Price: $5.95

Once again, Clifton presents a complex issue with the warmth and sensitivity needed by young readers. The illustrations by Grifalconi complement the text beautifully. In this story, Everett must adjust to a new stepfather, his mom's pregnancy, and a new baby. Just recently having introduced a new baby to the family, this reader has found a way (through this book) to broach the issue of change and new siblings.

The Faithful Friend
Author: Robert D. San Souci
Illustrator: Brian Pinkney
Publication Date: 1995
Price: $16.00

Having been raised in the same home, Clement and Hippolyte have developed a special bond of friendship that ties them as close as brothers. That bond is tested, however, as one friend must choose between his life or that of his friend. This fabulous tale of love and danger is set in the Caribbean island of Martinique. The illustrations, done by Pinkney, reflect the splendor and tropical beauty of that setting.

Flossie & the Fox
Author: Patricia C. McKissack
Illustrator: Rachel Isadora
Publication Date: 1986
Price: $14.99 (hardcover)

In this story that is quite reminiscent of the traditional Little Red Riding Hood, the wolf meets up with and is outsmarted by the intelligent and sassy Flossie. Set in American South and told in Black English Vernancular, this amusing tale is a joy to read.

Follow the Drinking Gourd
Author/Illustrator: Jeanette Winter
Publication Date: 1988
Price: $7.99

Not only does this book powerfully explain the Underground Railroad and the way in which enslaved Africans found freedom, it also exposes young readers to resistance efforts, hope, and an antiracist White role model, Peg Leg Joe, who helped many Blacks grasp liberty.

The Fortune-Tellers
Author: Lloyd Alexander
Illustrator: Trina Schart Hyman

Publication Date: 1992
Price: $15.00

A young carpenter visits a fortune-teller and he is thrilled to learn that his future will be promising. Returning to hear more promises, he finds the fortune-teller has disappeared. Thus, the carpenter assumes his role and the predictions of his future come true in an unusual way. The story, set in Cameroon, is beautifully illustrated through a variety of media, including ink, acrylic, and crayon. The beauty, strength, and diversity of the people and landscape are clearly displayed in the brilliant drawings.

Glorious Angels
Author: Walter Dean Myers
Publication Date: 1995
Price: $6.95

A sequel to *Brown Angels*, this book pairs eloquent poetry with magnificent antique photographs of children from around the world. Once again, the splendor and love of children is universally celebrated.

Grandfather's Journey
Author/Illustrator: Allen Say
Publication Date: 1993
Price: $16.95

Through compelling reminiscences of his grandfather's life in the United States and Japan, the author tells of his family's unique cross-cultural experiences. Like his grandfather, he too is torn between a love for two very different countries and a desire to be in both places simultaneously. The story is illustrated with beautiful paintings that tug at your heart with affection for both cultures. The nurturing relationship shared by the author and his grandfather is especially noteworthy.

Grandpa's Face
Author: Eloise Greenfield
Illustrator: Floyd Cooper
Publication Date: 1988
Price: $16.99 (paper)

Tamika and her grandfather share a special relationship. One day during Grandpa's play rehearsal, she sees a side of him that she's never seen before. As a result, Tamika becomes afraid that she will lose her grandfather's love one day. Perhaps one of this book's most distinguishing features is the wonderful illustrations. They are so vivid and realistic that they seem to leap off of the page.

The Handmade Alphabet
Author/Illustrator: Laura Rankin
Publication Date: 1991
Price: $14.99

The Handmade Alphabet introduces young children to the alphabet through the use of American Sign Language. This reader especially enjoyed the author/illustrator's use of multicultural hands and visual beauty of the illustrations. Even older children seem to enjoy this book and become actively engaged in trying to make the various signs with their hands.

I Like Me!
Author: Deborah Connor Coker
Illustrator: Keaf Holliday
Publication Date: 1995
Price: $2.80

Nia has a bright smile and an enthusiasm for everything she does. From ballet to running races, Nia enjoys herself and likes her life. She's versatile and cheerful. Children will like her instantly and identify with her genuine qualities.

I Love My Hair!
Author: Natasha Anastasia Tarpley
Illustrator: E. B. Lewis
Publication Date: 1998
Price: $14.95

Young Keyana loves the distinctiveness of her hair. She is able to wear it in braids, ponytails, or an afro. Her hair is a great source of pride for her and a reminder of her rich heritage.

Reproduced courtesy of Little, Brown and Company

Jamaica's Find
Author: Juanita Havill
Illustrator: Anne Sibley O'Brien
Publication Date: 1986
Price: $5.95

Jamaica finds a worn and seemingly much-loved stuffed animal in the park. She decides to keep him. With the help of her family, however, Jamaica learns lessons about loss and empathy. Ultimately, she must decide whether or not the toy shoud be returned.

Jamal's Busy Day
Author: Wade Hudson
Illustrator: George Ford
Publication Date: 1991
Price: $6.95

As Mom and Dad prepare for their respective days at work, Jamal gets ready for his job (school). Jamal compares his daily activities with his parents' routines. From breakfast, to school, to work and meetings, everyone looks forward to the return home and family time together at the end of the day. The illustrations in this book are bright, realistic, and complement the text. As part of the "Feeling Good" series, this book presents a very positive portrait of family life.

Jambo Means Hello: Swahili Alphabet Book
Author: Muriel Feelings
Illustrator: Tom Feelings
Publication Date: 1974
Price: $4.95 (paper)

Through a series of vivid and authentic illustrations, *Jambo Means Hello* introduces readers to Swahili words while simultaneously reinforcing the alphabet. Daily life in some parts of Africa, as well as African customs, are presented.

Jonathan and His Mommy
Author: Irene Smalls-Hector
Illustrator: Michael Hayes
Publication Date: 1994, 1992
Price: $4.95 (paper)

In this playful and entertaining story, a mother helps her young son explore their urban neighborhood. Mother and son play a simple game using a variety of steps, while simultaneously creating their own adventure. The language is poetic, while the illustrations are appealing and authentic.

Just Us Women
Author: Jeannette Caines
Illustrator: Pat Cummings
Publication Date: 1982
Price: $4.95

In this simple and straightforward tale, the young narrator and her Aunt Martha take a road trip to North Carolina in Aunt Martha's brand new car. Along the way, they encounter new and exciting adventures. The illustrations are absolutely stunning in their detail.

The Keeping Quilt
Author/Illustrator: Patricia Polacco
Publication Date: 1988
Price: $14.95

For four generations of a Jewish immigrant family, a quilt represents their individual lives, as well as symbolizes the family's collective love, strength, and faith. The passing down of the quilt from generation to generation reflects the cultural evolution of this family unit.

The Korean Cinderella
Author: Shirley Climo
Illustrator: Ruth Heller
Publication Date: 1993
Price: $15.00

Although this tale hails from Korea, it contains the elements apparent in Cinderella variants throughout the world. Cinderella, in the Korean version, is the beautiful Pear Blossom. Although she is given impossible chores to complete by her cruel stepmother, Omoni, Pear Blossom prevails with the aid of magic.

Let the Celebrations Begin!
Author: Margaret Wild
Illustrator: Julie Vivas
Publication Date: 1991
Price: $14.95 (hardcover)

Miriam lives in hut 18, bed 22. An adolescent, she remembers life at home prior to life in the concentration camp. With the other women, she makes toys out of scraps to give to the younger children at the very special party they are planning in anticipation that soldiers will arrive to liberate the camp. An extremely moving story, this one focuses not just on the atrocity of a holocaust, but it focuses on hope, resistance, and the power of the human spirit as well.

L'il Sis and Uncle Willie
Author: Gwen Everett
Paintings: William H. Johnson
Publication Date: 1991
Price: $4.95 (paper)

In this endearing story of love and admiration, a young girl recounts the visits of her worldly Uncle Willie. The story is based on the life of African American painter William H. Johnson (1901–1970). His artwork, which illustrates the book, is an introduction to one of the most recognized African American artists.

Lion Dancer: Ernie Wan's Chinese New Year
Authors: Kate Waters and Madeline Slovenz-Low
Photographer: Martha Cooper
Publication Date: 1990
Price: $13.95 (hardcover)

Ernie Wan provides young readers with a glimpse of his culture as he and his family prepare for Chinese New Year. Through this book, the reader accompanies Ernie as he gets ready to perform his first Lion Dance. The fabulous photographs presented throughout the book prove noteworthy.

Me and Neesie
Author: Eloise Greenfield
Publication Date: 1975
Price: $4.95 (paper)

Through her invisible friend Neesie, young Janell lives out her fears, joys, and life changes. Since most children have imaginary friends (at one point or the other), this reader believes that many will compare and relate Janell and Neesie's adventures to their own.

Mufaro's Beautiful Daughters
Author/Illustrator: John Steptoe
Publication Date: 1987
Price: $14.95 (hardcover)

Through the genre of fable, the story is told of Mufaro's two beautiful daughters, Manyara, who is ill-tempered, and Nyasha, who is sweet and kind. The two venture to go before the king who is attempting to choose a wife. Steptoe magnificently captures the essence of African culture and people. Based on the landscape of Zimbabwe and the faces of family members, Steptoe's illustrations are brought to life. The golden landscapes, fuschia skies, and emerald green forests created a vision of Africa in this reader's mind.

My Best Friend
Author: P. Mignon Hinds
Illustrator: Cornelius Van Wright
Publication Date: 1996
Price: $5.99 (hardcover)

Omar and his best friend don't always get along. Most of the time, however, they do. They sometimes disagree, but their friendship is important to them. Young readers will learn that it is okay for best friends to have differences.

My Little Island
Author/Illustrator: Frane Lessac
Publication Date: 1994
Price: $6.95 (paper)

A young boy and his friend, Lucca, travel to the Caribbean island on which he was born. The life and customs of this small island are explored through their journeys. One of this book's most distinguishing features is the use of brilliant color. Scarlet reds, mandarin oranges, and crystal blues catch the detail and splendor of the Caribbean.

My Painted House, My Friendly Chicken and Me
Author: Maya Angelou
Photographer: Margaret Courtney-Clarke
Publication Date: 1994
Price: $6.99 (paper)

This wonderful book explores the rich culture and tradition of the small South African village of Ndebele through the eyes of eight-year-old Thandi. Thandi lives with her mother, her aunts, her brother, and her best friend, a chicken. Angelou's prose and Courtney-Clarke's photos truly capture the wonderful, aesthetic beauty of the small village. The combination of the two elements enabled this reader to experience the art, culture, and social dimensions of Ndebele, from an insightful, fresh perspective.

The Patchwork Quilt
Author: Valerie Flournoy
Illustrator: Jerry Pinkney
Publication Date: 1985
Price: $13.95 (hardcover)

By helping her grandmother make a family quilt, young Tanya comes to realize that the quilt is more than a simple blanket. It is a representation of her family history. The wonderful watercolors used in this book's illustrations aptly depict the characters' individuality and sense of self through the use of diverse hair styles, hair colors, and skin hues. A strong family bond is further expressed and the family unit is esteemed in this loving portrait.

Pink and Say
Author/Illustrator: Patricia Polacco
Publication Date: 1994
Price: $15.95 (hardcover)

In this story, Sheldon Say, a young White soldier, becomes acquainted with Pinkus Aylee, a young Black soldier, during the Civil War. Both naive and afraid of war's disastrous effects, they become strong friends. Eventually, Say is nursed back to health by Pink's mother. Even though Pink and Say respond to each other as equals, societal racism distinguishes. The story is retold by Sheldon's ancestors as a tribute to Pinkus Aylee, who helped to save Say's life.

Rechenka's Eggs
Author/Illustrator: Patricia Polacco
Publication Date: 1998
Price: $5.95 (paper)

Babushka is known for the fine eggs she paints, and she always wins first prize at the Easter Festival in Moskva. One day, she rescues an injured goose, Rechenka. While nursing it back to health, Rechenka accidentally breaks the painted eggs intended for the festival. To Babushka's amazement, Rechenka lays 13 marvelously colored eggs and leaves behind one final miracle before returning to her flock. This is an endearing story of Babushka's love of art, animals, and the miracle of life. This story was read to a first-grade class by this reader. They loved Babushka's talent and kindness, but marveled over Rechenka's miracle eggs.

The Rough Faced Girl
Author: Rafe Martin
Illustrator: David Shannon
Publication Date: 1992
Price: $14.95

This book is derived from the Algonquin variant of the Cinderella tale. In fact, this version of the story is one of the oldest in existence. In this variation, an Invisible Being will marry the first maiden who can see him. The rough faced girl, so named for the scars and burns she incurs from tending the fires, decides that she too can attempt to win the Invisible Being's heart.

See Me Grow, Head to Toe!
Author: Nanette Van Wright Mellage
Illustrator: Keaf Holliday
Publication Date: 1996
Price: $2.69 (paper)

Children will enjoy the rhyming text and beautiful, smiling faces of toddlers as they explore the world around them. The story will also familiarize them with the various parts of the body.

She Come Bringing Me That Little Baby Girl
Author: Eloise Greenfield
Illustrator: John Steptoe
Publication Date: 1974
Price: $6.95

When Kevin's parents bring a new baby home, he feels all of the jealousy and resentment usually associated with sibling rivalry. With time, however, he comes to the realization that his parents will never stop loving him and that he will now take on a significant, new role in the family . . . big brother. Kevin's feelings are vividly expressed through language that a young child might use in everyday conversations.

The Story of Ruby Bridges
Author: Robert Coles
Illustrator: George Ford
Publication Date: 1995
Price: $14.95 (hardcover)

Based on a true story, this picture storybook shares the story of a little first-grade girl placed in the position of integrating an all-White school in New Orleans during the tumultuous 1960s. The inner strength that this youngster possessed is both haunting and uncanny. She appears nearly unaffected by the negativity that surrounds her. She is able to move forward, in spite of threats, jeers, and harassment.

The Snowy Day
Author/Illustrator: Ezra Jack Keats
Publication Date: 1962
Price: $5.99 (paper)

Young Peter awakens in the morning to discover a snowfall. He can't wait to get outside and turn his day into an adventure. He climbs, makes snowballs, angels, and finally tries to capture a piece of the day by saving a snowball in his pocket.

Sootface: An Ojibwa Cinderella Story
Author: Robert D. San Souci
Illustrator: Daniel San Souci
Publication Date: 1994
Price: $14.95

Sootface is so named because her cruel sisters force her to tend the cooking fires that singe her face, hair, and arms. One day, however, Sootface learns that the Invisible Hunter has decreed that he will marry the maiden who is able to meet his challenge—she can see him. Despite her appearance and the taunts of her sisters and fellow villagers, Sootface journeys to the hunter's home to find the love of which she dreams. This version of Cinderella seems to mirror Martin's *The Rough Faced Girl*, based on the Algonquin tale. Sootface, like the rough faced girl, relies on her inner beauty and courage.

Sukey and the Mermaid
Author: Robert D. San Souci
Illustrator: Brian Pinkney

Publication Date: 1992
Price: $14.95 (hardcover)

One warm afternoon, Sukey ecapes from her abusive stepfather, Mister Jones, to the water's edge upon which she sings a song she has heard. In response to the song, Mama Jo (a mermaid) appears. The friendship between Mama Jo and Sukey alters both lives permanently. This story is based on an early African American folktale about mermaids. The illustrations vividly capture its magical setting. Readers of all ages will enjoy this tale.

Sweet Clara and the Freedom Quilt
Author: Deborah Hopkinson
Illustrator: James Ransome
Publication Date: 1993
Price: $15.00

Slavery has separated Clara from her mother, but she is determined to reunite with her one day and escape North to freedom. As a seamstress, Clara is recruited to sew a "freedom quilt," which ultimately serves as a map and guides Clara and other slaves to freedom. Clara's resourcefulness and courage make this story an inspirational and educational chapter in African American history.

Talking Walls
Author: Margery Burns Knight
Illustrator: Anne Sibley O'Brien
Publication Date: 1992
Price: $8.95

This book describes different cultures by focusing on walls around the world. The impact of partitions, such as the Great Wall of China and the Berlin Wall, are explored. Also, the compendium provided at the end of the book is filled with additional background information on the respective walls.

Reproduced courtesy of Tilbury House, Publishers.

Tar Beach
Author/Illustrator: Faith Ringgold
Publication Date: 1996
Price: $6.99 (paper)

Young Cassie's vivid imagination enables her to fly. Her flight allows her to own pieces of New York City, which she generously shares with her family. Her fantastic travels and magic powers allow her to fondly recount times spent with family and friends on "tar beach," in addition to potentially righting the wrongs of discrimination and racism.

Teammates
Author: Peter Golenbock
Publication Date: 1990
Price: $14.95 (hardcover)

This book focuses on the racial discrimination endured by Jackie Robinson as the first Black man to enter major league baseball and the special relationship he shared with his Euro-American Brooklyn Dodgers' teammate, Pee Wee Reese. This reader shared this book with her 93–year-old grandfather. As they flipped through the pages of the book, the photographs triggered the grandfather's recollections and feelings of that era. He recalled news stories and Robinson's first game as a Dodger. The integration of illustrations, actual headlines, baseball cards, and photographs made the topic of racial prejudice more tangible. Also, exploring prejudice in a familiar context, such as baseball, allows children to connect and relate to the subject concretely.

Tell Me a Story, Mama
Author: Angela Johnson
Illustrations: David Soman
Publication Date: 1989
Price: $6.95 (paper)

A young girl loves to hear stories of Mama growing up, whether she was getting into mischief or finding a puppy. She likes these tales so much that she finishes them for Mama. Fortunately, Mama doesn't mind. This engaging story emphasizes the bond between parent and child, as well as the importance of passing the oral tradition from one generation to the next.

Through Moon and Stars and Night Skies
Author: Ann Turner
Publication Date: 1990
Price: $14.00

This book describes a young Asian boy's journey from a far away land to his new adoptive home in the United States. Although he initially has feelings of uncertainty and apprehension, he learns that his new family brings love and acceptance. As a result, the subject of adoption is approached with warmth, sensitivity, and dignity.

The True Story of the Three Little Pigs
Author: Jon Scieszka
Illustrator: Lane Smith
Publication Date: 1989
Price: $14.95 (hardcover)

In this hilarious version of *The Three Little Pigs*, A. Wolf gets to tell his side of the story. According to him, his bad image is the fault of the media.

Uncle Jed's Barbershop
Author: Margaree King Mitchell
Illustrator: James Ransome
Publication Date: 1993
Price: $5.99

Uncle Jed was Sarah Jean's favorite uncle and the only Black barber in the county. After cutting her dad's and granddad's hair, Uncle Jed would pretend to cut hers. He also told Sarah Jean of his dream . . . to one day save enough money to purchase his own barbershop. His dream is actualized. Uncle Jed finally has enough money for his barbershop. Unfortunately, he must use his savings to assist during a family crisis that involves Sarah Jean. Through Uncle Jed, she learns about commitment, love, hard work, and sacrifice.

Welcoming Babies
Author: Margy Burns Knight
Illustrator: Anne Sibley O'Brien
Publication Date: 1995
Price: $14.95 (hardcover)

Universally, babies seem to bring joy. In this wonderful book, Knight takes the reader around the world to see the ways in which new life is affirmed and babies are welcomed.

Reproduced courtesy of Tilbury House, Publishers.

What I Want to Be
Author: P. Mignon Hinds
Illustrator: Cornelius Van
  Wright
Publication Date: 1995
Price: $4.76 (hardcover)

Reproduced courtesy of Essence Books for Children.

Maya loves to visit her grandmother. She has fun rummaging through an old trunk. Everything she finds reminds her of something she might want to be when she grows up. From archaeologist to underwater scientist to firefighter to dress designer, Maya imagines herself busy at work. Her grandmother reminds her that she can be whatever she chooses, but she should always do her personal best.

What Mary Jo Shared
Author: Janice May Udry
Illustrator: Elizabeth Sayles
Publication Date: 1991, 1966
Price: $4.99 (paper)

Shy Mary Jo tries diligently to work up the nerve to share something different from the other children in her class for show-and-tell. Each time she decides on something, another student seems to get the same idea. Finally, Mary Jo decides to share one of her most prized and valued possessions.

When I Am Old with You
Author: Angela Johnson
Illustrator: David Soman
Publication Date: 1990
Price: $5.95 (paper)

A young child relishes the time spent with a grandparent in this richly drawn portrait of intergenerational love. Soman's fabulous watercolor illustrations add to the sense of warmth and sincerity that one receives from Johnson's text.

When I Was Young in the Mountains
Author: Cynthia Rylant
Illustrator: Diane Goode
Publication Date: 1982
Price: $4.99

Life in Appalachia is made real for young readers as the young narrator shares the time she spends with her grandparents. She walks through cow pastures, accompanies her grandmother to the johnny-house, and attends church in the schoolhouse.

White Rabbit's Color Book
Author/Illustrator: Alan Baker
Publication Date: 1994
Price: $7.95

White Rabbit not only introduces toddlers and preschoolers to colors, he also familiarizes them with the colors produced from diverse mixtures of colors. This reader's child finds it interesting enough to read again and again.

INTERMEDIATE CHAPTER BOOKS

The Best Bad Thing
Author: Yoshiko Uchida
Publication Date: 1983
Price: $4.95

Twelve-year-old Rinko must spend the summer with her mother's eccentric friend Mrs. Hata. To Rinko, helping the recently widowed Mrs. Hata is a bad thing, especially during summer vacaction. Yet, during her stay, Rinko learns valuable lessons about compassion, acceptance, and self-sacrifice.

Felita
Author: Nicholasa Mohr
Illustrator: Ray Cruz
Publication Date: 1979
Price: $3.99

After a brief move to a "better" neighborhood, Felita and her family experience racism and violence. How does one respond to racism? There are many different approaches and the family selects one. They return to the familiar sights, sounds, family, and friends of the old neighborhood. Family, community and the sense of belonging are all central themes of this story.

A Gift for Tia Rosa
Author: Karen T. Taha
Illustrator: Dee deRosa
Publication Date: 1986
Price: $3.50

Tia Rosa has been teaching young Carmela to knit. The two sit side-by-side and complete their projects. Then, Tia Rosa falls ill. Although Tia returns, she isn't the same. Yet, in the limited time she has, she shares some very important life lessons with her young friend.

The Gift Giver
Author: Joyce Hansen
Publication Date: 1980
Price: $6.95 (paper)

After reading this book, readers will share a understanding of the ways in which the qualities of friendship, patience, and tolerance will enhance their lives. The plot revolves around Doris, a fifth grader, who lives in the Bronx and befriends a boy, Amir, living in a neighborhood foster home. These two special children learn from, as well as give to, each other. The story is realistically told and destined to evoke emotion.

How it Feels to Live with a Physical Disability
Author/Photographer: Jill Krementz
Publication Date: 1992
Price: $18.00 (hardcover)

In a sensitive and uncompromising presentation, Krementz introduces readers to an extraordinary group of young people who are coping with various physical disabilities. Each chapter is written in a member of the group's own words, and the beautiful photos show each child engaged in diverse daily activities.

Justin and the Best Biscuits in the World
Author: Mildred Pitts Walter
Publication Date: 1986
Price: $3.99

Justin lives in a home with his mother and two sisters. While his mother and sister Hadiya seem to understand him, his eldest sister Evelyn seems to think that he can't do anything right. Fortunately, Justin's grandfather comes to the resuce. He takes the boy for a vacation at his home. There Justin learns to cook and make his bed; but most important, he gains self-confidence and self-acceptance.

Number the Stars
Author: Lois Lowry
Publication Date: 1989
Price: $3.50 (paper)

Number the Stars chronicles Annemarie Johansen and her family's struggle to help Jews escape Nazi-occupied Denmark during World War II. Annemarie bravely goes on a dangerous mission to save her best friend's life. This book had a powerful effect on this reader and she couldn't stop thinking about it for days. Both the courage and vulnerability of Annemarie were admired. Through Lowry's powerful writing, the heroine took on a life of her own. She did not remain a mere character in a book.

Phoebe the Spy
Author: Judith Berry Griffin
Publication Date: 1977
Price: $2.75

During the American Revolution, a young Phoebe is sent to General George Washington's home to discover the identity of the man planning to kill him. Phoebe, frightened and unsure, watches and listens, ultimately saving General Washinton's life. Phoebe's courage and initiative should prove inspirational for all children.

Sadako and the Thousand Paper Cranes
Author: Eleanor Coerr
Publication Date: 1977
Price: $3.50 (paper)

Sadako was two years old when Hiroshima was bombed. Ten years later, while running, she collapses. After several medical tests, Sadako is diagnosed with leukemia that resulted from her exposure to the bomb's radiation. This short biographical portrait tells of her illness and her belief in a friend's pronouncement that if she is able to fold a thousand paper cranes, her life will be spared. This story's heroine, Sadako Sasaki, is a heroine to children in Japan. In honor of her courage and faith, a statue of Sadako stands in the Hiroshima Peace Park.

Shiloh
Author: Phyllis Reynolds Naylor
Publication Date: 1991
Price: $4.99

When 11–year-old Marty discovers a mistreated beagle, he decides to keep the dog. His parents, however, insist that he return it to its abusive owner. Marty disobeys and hides the dog from both his parents and the owner. As a result, a near tragedy occurs. *Shiloh* is not simply a story about a boy and a dog, it is a complex tale of moral dilemmas that confront us all. Much like authors Taylor and Woodson, Naylor does not provide readers with simplistic answers to life's most difficult questions. Instead, she asks questions through her characters that lead the reader to deeper questions.

YOUNG ADULT

All Times, All People: A World History of Slavery
Author: Milton Meltzer
Illustrator: Leonard Everett Fisher
Publication Date: 1980
Price: $21.95 (hardcover)

All Times, All People is a highly readable text on slavery throughout the world and ages. Meltzer traces slavery from Egypt and its enslavement of the Israelites to the United States and its enslavement of Africans. Meltzer also aptly discusses resistance efforts to slavery and presents the enslaved in a compassionate and dignified light. This book could be used as a companion volume to Lester's *To Be a Slave*.

A Hero Ain't Nothin but a Sandwich
Author: Alice Childress
Publication Date: 1973
Price: $4.50 (paper)

Thirteen-year-old Benjie and those who love him give a heart-wrenching account of his heroine addiction. Although Benjie is confident that he can kick his habit, others doubt that change will come so easily. The blatantly truthful manner in which the story is told immediately captures the reader and keeps her or him engaged throughout.

Baseball in April and Other Stories
Author: Gary Soto
Publication Date: 1990
Price: $6.00

Baseball in April and Other Stories is a collection of 11 short stories depicting the daily lives of Mexican American youth growing up in California. The stories focus on family, friends, school, and the pangs of first love. Soto presents this world with both humor and sensitivity. Each story transcends cultural boundaries, enabling readers to see themselves in similar situations. At the end of the book, there is a helpful glossary of Spanish words and phrases that were used in the stories.

Christmas in the Big House, Christmas in the Quarters
Authors: Patricia and Frederick McKissack
Illustrator: John Thompson
Publication Date: 1994
Price: $15.95

Christmas will never be the same for either the enslaved Africans living in the quarters or their Euro-American "owners" who reside in the Big House as the Civil War rapidly approaches and the institution of slavery is challenged. The McKissacks do an exemplary job of contrasting life for those who are enslaved and those who enslave them. They subtly send a powerful message about slavery to young readers. The illustrations are exquisite, as well.

The Dear One
Author: Jacqueline Woodson
Publication Date: 1991
Price: $3.50

Twelve-year-old Afeni, a Swahili name that means "dear one," is coping with her parents' divorce and her grandmother's death when her mother informs her that a college friend's 15-year-old daughter will be living with them until the girl delivers her baby. Afeni is angry that she will have to share both her mother and her bedroom with Rebecca. *The Dear One* is a textured novel that illuminates the differences between Afeni's suburban life and Rebecca's urban one, as well as broaches the topic of teen pregnancy in a thoughtful and realistic manner.

The Friendship/The Gold Cadillac
Author: Mildred Taylor
Publication Date: 1989
Price: $2.95 (paper)

In the first of the two novellas, *The Friendship*, elderly Mr. Tom Bee refuses to disregard the pact he and White store owner John Wallace made long ago. Unfortunately, his refusal has grave consequences. In *The Gold Cadillac*, a car is the catalyst for family discord and racism. Both stories are powerful and memorable.

From the Notebooks of Melanin Sun
Author: Jacqueline Woodson
Publication Date: 1995
Price: $3.99 (paper)

Melanin Sun (Mel for short) is going through the things that most young teens his age encounter, until he discovers that his mother is a lesbian. Although he and his mom have always been close and relied on each other, he now has to cope with the stereotypes perpetuated about and ignorance surrounding the issue of homosexuality. He also has to deal with his feelings about race because his mother's lover is a White woman. This book does not offer easy answers to life's many questions. Instead, it offers readers authentic situations and people who struggle to do the best they can.

The Giver
Author: Lois Lowry
Publication Date: 1993
Price: $5.50 (paper)

Imagine a society in which there is no pain or poverty and citizens have no choice. Jobs are assigned on the basis of ability. This is the world in which 12-year-old Jonas lives. Recently assigned the prestigious job of "receiver of memories," Jonas is responsible for maintaining all the memories of past existences so that others might be spared the pain and suffering of knowledge. Yet, surprise is in store as Jonas and his mentor decide that it's time for a change.

Hiroshima No Pika
Author: T. Maruki
Publication Date: 1980
Price: $16.00

In this stirring account of the U.S. bombing of Hiroshima, an eyewitness describes the sights and sounds of that fateful day. A powerful and intense story of tragedy and destruction that will leave an impression on almost any reader.

I Hadn't Meant to Tell You This
Author: Jacqueline Woodson
Publication Date: 1994
Price: $3.99 (paper), $14.95 (hardcover)

In an interesting reversal for children's and adolescent fiction, Marie (a popular, middle class Black girl) forms an unlikely friendship with a poor and troubled White girl named Lena. The loss of their mothers draws the girls to each other and helps them to support one another through trying times. One of those trying times, however, threatens to destroy the relationship they share. This reader remembers someone once saying that a good book leaves its reader wanting more. In this case, Woodson's book did just that.

The Journey: Japanese Americans, Racism and Renewal
Author/Illustrator: Sheila Hamanaka
Publication Date: 1990
Price: $18.95

Inspired by a 25-foot mural, this absorbing book focuses on Japanese immigration to the United States and the subsequent internment of Japanese Americans during World War II. It features a stunning visual display and focuses on a chapter of American history with which many are unfamiliar.

Journey to Jo'burg: A South African Story
Author: Beverly Naidoo
Publication date: 1986
Price: $4.95 (paper)

Determined to find their mother and inform her of their baby sister's grave illness, Naledi and her younger brother, Tiro, journey from their small South African village to the metropolis of Johannesburg. The excursion results in a number of revelations about apartheid and the realities associated with life as Black South Africans during a time of siege.

Kids at Work: Lewis Hine and the Crusade Against Child Labor
Author: Russell Freedman

Photographs: Lewis W. Hine
Publication Date: 1994
Price: $16.95

During the early 1900s and as industrialization transformed American society, children were widely used for labor in factories, mills, mines, and fields across the United States. Conditions were horrible, but the children's families needed the additional wages for mere survival. Lewis W. Hine, teacher and photographer, felt so strongly about the abuse of this practice that he became an investigative reporter for the National Child Labor Committee. Through the distribution of his photos, he convinced people that the United States needed laws that would protect children from being used, to their own detriment, as cheap labor.

Leon's Story
Author: Leon Walter Tillage
Collage Art: Susan Roth
Publication Date: 1997
Price: $14.00

This autobiography's genesis came about in a distinctive fashion. Artist Roth's child came home and told her of the fascinating story her school's janitor revealed during assembly. Roth decided to encourage Tillage to document his story and share it with other young people. This book, that chronicles the strong bond of family and human spirit amid racial intolerance and injustice, is the end result.

Lest We Forget: The Passage from Africa to Slavery and Emancipation
Compiled by: Vilma Maia Thomas
Publication Date: 1997
Price: $29.95 (hardcover)

The history of slavery is brought to life in a new and intriguing way through this collection of text and images. Through the use of this interactive volume, the reader is provided the opportunity to see and touch reproduced artifacts that were authentic to the slave trade. Additionally, the horrors of slavery are made real and concrete for young readers.

Like Sisters on the Homefront
Author: Rita Williams-Garcia
Publication Date: 1995
Price: $4.99 (paper)

When 14-year-old Gayle becomes pregnant for the second time, her mother decides that Gayle should leave the city. Mama sends Gayle and her seven-month-old son, Jose, to her brother, a minister, and his family in Georgia. Through richly developed characters, Williams-Garcia touches on issues of family, friendship, teen pregnancy, abortion, and religion.

Lincoln: A Photobiography
Author: Russell Freedman
Publication Date: 1987
Price: $7.95

With exquisite detail and artistry, Freedman captures the complexity of President Abraham Lincoln. He shows Lincoln' s frailties, as well as his strengths. He also enables young readers to understand Lincoln's true beliefs about slavery, the emancipation of slaves, and the Civil War. Much of this is conveyed in his own words.

Many Thousand Gone: African Americans from Slavery to Freedom
Author: Virginia Hamilton
Illustrators: Leo and Diane Dillon
Publication Date: 1993
Price: $16.00 (hardcover)

In this beautifully illustrated chronicle, Hamilton outlines the history of slavery in the United States. In fascinating detail, she tells of the slave trade and Underground Railroad and privileges the life narratives of the enslaved.

The Middle Passage: White Ships Black Cargo
Illustrator: Tom Feelings
Introduction: Dr. John Henrik Clark
Publication Date: 1995
Price: $45.00 (hardcover)

Any reader, adult or child, will be mesmerized by the beauty and suffering that Feelings brings together in this picture book outlining the transport of enslaved Africans from their native land and through a horrific transatlantic voyage. Feelings's haunting black and white illustrations brilliantly depict the emotions of the enslaved, as well as share the anguish of their capture and their heroic efforts to resist the bondage of their oppressors.

Mississippi Bridge
Author: Mildred Taylor
Publication Date: 1990
Price: $3.50 (paper)

On a rainy day in 1930's Mississippi and during Jim Crow segregation, Josias Williams and Grandmother Logan are ordered from a bus to make room for arriving White passengers. Shortly after, a tragic event occurs. In this powerful and disturbing tale, the reader is left to ponder the effects of discrimination and its moral implications.

Now Is Your Time!: The African American Struggle for Freedom
Author: Walter Dean Myers
Publication Date: 1991
Price: $10.95

In this impressive volume, Myers documents the struggle of African Americans from their rough voyage during the Middle Passage to the 1960s' Civil Rights Movement. Myers masterfully records the events and people that have shaped our futures and helped to determine our destinies here in the United States.

The People Could Fly: American Black Folktales
Author: Virginia Hamilton
Illustrators: Diane and Leo Dillon
Publication Date: 1993
Price: $13.00 (paper)

In this fine collection of folktales, Virginia Hamilton captures the essence of Black humor, triumph, and lessons to be passed from one generation to the next. The tales, simply expressed, will appeal to readers of all ages. The elegantly drawn illustrations, done in black and white, assist in bringing each such carefully crafted tale to life.

Roll of Thunder, Hear My Cry
Author: Mildred Taylor
Publication Date: 1976
Price: $2.95

Nine-year-old Cassie Logan narrates the story of her family during one year in Depression-era Mississippi. The events encompass school, a wayward friend, and the start of a cooperative. At the heart of these events is the racism that confronts the Logans on a daily basis, each family member's individual and varied response, and the family's resolve to remain strong and viable. Taylor's understated writing belies the power of Cassie's story and will leave readers pensive regarding the issues addressed and the ways in which they would respond or have responded in similar situations.

Scorpions
Author: Walter Dean Myers
Publication Date: 1988
Price: $4.50

While Randy is in prison, he wants his 12-year-old brother, Jamal, to lead his gang, the Scorpions. Lured by the money that running drugs could bring for Randy's appeal, Jamal reluctantly accepts the position. Yet, as the leader of the gang, Jamal is given a gun that forever changes the lives of both Jamal and his best friend, Tito. In *Scorpions*, Myers does not glorify the inherent violence of gangs. Instead, he has crafted a sensitive and provocative story about young boys who must accept responsibility for their actions. Similar to his other books, this novel by Myers invites serious dialogue.

The Shimmershine Queens
Author: Camille Yarbrough
Publication Date: 1989
Price: $3.50

Ten-year-old Angie has to cope with classmates who pick on her, a mother who is depressed, and the other pressures associated with simply being a child. It seems like things will never get any better until Cousin Seatta arrives and shares some words of wisdom. Those simple words about self-love and pride in one's heritage change Angie's entire outlook on life. It might prove beneficial for parents to peruse this book first as some object to the language used.

A Short Walk Around the Pyramids & Through the World of Art
Author: Philip Isaacson
Publication Date: 1993
Price: $25.00

This book is one of the most interesting this reader has viewed in regard to exposing young people to the world of art. Isaacson does a comprehensive and apt job of taking the reader around the world to enjoy the artistic contributions of diverse cultures, in addition to demystifying a complex topic.

Somewhere in the Darkness
Author: Walter Dean Myers
Publication Date: 1992
Price: $3.99 (paper)

One afternoon, 14-year-old Jimmy returns home from school and discovers Crab, his absentee father, waiting for him. Curious to know his father, who was imprisoned when he was an infant, Jimmy accompanies Crab to Chicago, where Crab claims a job awaits him. Jimmy learns some difficult lessons about life, love, and honesty along the way. The relationship between father and son is central to this book.

Stitching Stars
Author: Mary E. Lyons
Publication Date: 1993
Price: $6.99

As a biography of African American quilter, Harriet Powers's life, the history of quilting, and its significance is explored. Through this book, the reader learned as much about the art of quilting as she did about the life history of Harriet Powers. For women like Powers, each quilt served as a story being retold. The craftsmanship and beauty captured the folktales and religious stories told through the quilts.

To Be a Slave
Author: Julius Lester
Publication Date: 1968
Price: $2.75 (paper)

Compiled from various sources and carefully documented, this book chronicles the lives of enslaved Africans in their own words. Each of the seven chapters focuses on distinct experiences, such as the auction block, resistance to slavery, and emancipation. Lester's commentaries are unassuming, allowing the personal stories to speak for themselves.

Toning the Sweep
Author: Angela Johnson
Publication Date: 1993
Price: $3.99

Three generations of Black women come together, while each holds on to a separate truth about life, death, and themselves. Emmie and her mother, Diane, travel to the desert to bring her grandmother back home with them. Ola, however, is suffering from terminal cancer. During the trip, Emmie comes to the end of her childhood, the beginning of womanhood, the connection that exists in families, and the power of friendship.

Young, Black and Determined: A Biography of Lorraine Hansberry
Authors: Patricia and Frederick McKissack
Publication Date: 1998
Price: $18.95

In this skillfully done biography, the McKissacks present a loving and dignified portrait of Lorraine Hansberry, Black intellectual and advocate for social justice. This reader was particularly impressed with the research that obviously shaped this book and the high regard with which the McKissacks apparently hold their young readers.

Appendix B:
Selection Process for List
of Suggested Books

I feel certain that I would not be a published writer if my mother had not told me the following: "Read, read well and read to understand. If you can read, you can do anything, because what others have created or accomplished has been written about. If you go to the library, you will find information to inspire you and guide you to accomplish anything you want to do."

I took her words to heart and still do. Whenever I am starting a project, the first place I go is the library. What a wonderful place it is!

—Anita R. Bunkley, Author
(as quoted in Tamara Nikuradse's
*My Mother had a Dream: African-American
Women Share Their Mothers' Words of Wisdom)*

The list of children's and adolescent books compiled in Appendix A is representative of a collective effort rather than an individual decision. The determination was predicated on the assumption that a diversity of voices and perspectives would strengthen the quality of the list, while concomitantly enriching the evaluative experience of group participants. In a sense, I (as the author) held the view that both new and experienced eyes were needed in the assessment of books for inclusion.

As a result, a group consisting of four teachers (with varying levels of experience reviewing children's and adolescent literature), a librarian, and I met several times during the academic semester, Spring 1998.

Three of the participants were Black and three were White; five of us were women and one was a man. The group seemed to characterize our meetings as cordial and informative. We seemed to have a good working relationship, and a number of group members specifically referred to their beliefs that all voices were equally respected and valued.

Prior to meeting times, group participants were asked to read books for potential inclusion and to make recommendations. Typically, two group members would read and recommend the same book before it was seriously considered. There were many times during which we were all in agreement about the artistry reflected in a particular book. There were other times during which our opinions differed. On such occasions, those who were familiar with the selection discussed the book's strengths and weaknesses. We also asked the librarian if children were actually requesting the book in question. Subsequently, we voted. With relatively few exceptions, we reached some type of consensus on all of the books contained within Appendix A. All the books included do not contain Black characters. We felt that there were stories and experiences presented by other groups that were equally important to the human experience. Thus, we desired to share them. Also, in our collective estimation, the books that appear on our list represent the very best that children's literature has to offer.

Book annotations were divided among us. Thus, most of us participated in writing them. Some read the books with their respective classes, students, and families and noted their reactions, in addition to our own.

I am quite pleased with the group's effort and the fruit of our labor; yet, I fully realize that I am solely responsible for this book's content. Any omissions or questionable choices were based on sound rationales and approved by me.

Appendix C:
Stereotypes Worksheet

GENDER STEREOTYPES

Male

active

brave

strong

rough

competitive

inventive

intelligent, logical

quiet, easygoing

decisive, problem-solving

messy

tall

mechanical

independent

leader, innovator

expressing anger

unemotional

playing or working outdoors

unconcerned about appearance

as parent, playing with children

having innate need for adventure

Female

passive
frightened
weak
gentle
giving up easily
unoriginal
silly, illogical
shrewish, nagging
confused
neat
short
inept
dependent
follower, conformist
controlling anger
emotional
playing and working indoors
concerned about appearance
as parent, nurturing children
having innate need for marriage and motherhood

STEROTYPES OF ASIAN AMERICANS

Male

smiling, polite, and small
servile and bowing
bucktoothed and squinty-eyed
mystical, inscrutable, and wise
expert in martial arts
exotic foreigner
sinister, sly
places no value on human life
model minority who worked hard and "made it"
super-student

Female

sweet, well-behaved girl

sexy, sweet "China Doll"

sexy, evil "Dragon Lady"

overbearing, old-fashioned grandmother

STEREOTYPES OF BLACKS

Male

the shuffling, eye-rolling, fearful, superstitious comic

the gentle, self-sacrificing older man

the athletic super-jock

the super-stud

the stupid, but comical, little boy

the rough, dangerous criminal

the loudly dressed, happy-go-lucky buffoon

the exotic primitive

Female

the big-breasted "mammy," loyal to whites

the big, bossy mother or maid—commander of the household

the sexy temptress

the stupid, but sweet, little girl

the tragic mulatto

STEREOTYPES OF LATINOS

Male

sombrero-wearing, serape-clad, sandaled man or boy

man taking a siesta near a cactus or an overburdened burro

ignorant, cheerful, lazy peon

sneaky, knife-wielding, mustached bandit

humble, big-eyed, poor-but-honest boy

teenage gang member

macho boaster and supreme-commander of household

Female

hard-working, poor, submissive, self-sacrificing mother of many

sweet, small, shy, gentle girl

sexy, loud, fiery, young woman (who often prefers White men to Latino men)

undereducated, submissive, nice girl with marriage as a life goal

Occupational

impoverished migrant workers (most Latinos actually live in cities)
unemployed barrio dwellers

STEREOTYPES OF NATIVE AMERICANS

Male

savage, bloodthirsty "native"
stoic, loyal follower
drunken, mean thief
hunter, tracker
noble child of nature
wise old chief
evil medicine man
brave boy, endowed with special "Indian" qualities

Female

heavyset, workhorse "squaw"
"Indian princess" (depicted with European features and often in love with a
    White man for whom she is willing to sacrifice her life)

Occupational

hunters
cattle thieves
warriors
unemployed loafers
craftspeople

STEREOTYPES OF DIFFERENTLY ABLED PEOPLE

Male

evil blind man with unnatural powers
village "idiot"
evil "peg-leg" or "hook arm"
pitiful paraplegic
ugly "hunchback"
deaf and "dumb" sad character
super "cripple"
pitiful little "cripple"

childlike dwarf
"insane" criminal
one-eyed pirate
"hard of hearing" crank

Female

"hunchbacked" old crone
blind witch
pitiful blind girl
pitiful, little cripple
sexless, sad creature
victim of violence
evil witch with a cane
self-pitying whiner

Appendix D: Ten Quick Ways to Analyze Children's Books for Sexism and Racism

The following ten guidelines are offered as a starting point in the evaluation of children's/adolescent books.

1. CHECK THE ILLUSTRATIONS

Look for Stereotypes

A stereotype is an oversimplified generalization about a particular group, race, gender, class, sexual orientation, and so forth, which usually carries derogatory implications. Some infamous (overt) stereotypes of Blacks are happy-go-lucky, watermelon-eating Sambo, and the fat, eye-rolling "Mammy"; of Chicanos, the sombrero-wearing peon or the fiesta-loving, macho bandito; of Asian Americans, the inscrutable, slant-eyed "Oriental"; of Native Americans, the naked savage or "primitive" craftsperson and his squaw; of Puerto Ricans, the switchblade-toting, teenage gang member; of women, the completely domesticated mother, the demure, doll-loving little girl or the wicked stepmother. As times have changed, stereotypes have become less blatant. Yet, one should be cautious of variations that in any way demean or ridicule characters because of their race, gender, or other characteristics.

Look for Tokenism

If there are characters of color in the illustrations, do they look just like whites except for being tinted or colored in? Do all ethnic faces look stereotypically alike, or are they depicted as genuine individuals with distinctive features?

Who's Doing What?

Do the illustrations depict people of color in subservient or passive roles or in leadership and action roles? Are males the active "doers" and females the inactive observers? Are illustrations of male characters larger and more prominent than those of females? Are white characters featured higher on the page than characters of color?

2. CHECK THE STORY LINE

The liberation movements of the 1960s have led publishers to remove many insulting passages, particularly from stories with Black themes and from books depicting female characters; however, racist and sexist attitudes still find expression in less obvious ways. The following are several examples.

Standards for Success

Does it take "White" behavior standards for a person of color to "get ahead?" Is "making it" in the dominant White society projected as the only ideal? To gain acceptance and approval, do third-world persons have to exhibit extraordinary qualities—excel in sports, get good grades, for example? In friendships between White children and children of color, does the child of color do most of the understanding and forgiving?

Resolution of Problems

How are the problems presented, conceived, and resolved in the story? Are people of color considered "the problem?" Are the oppressions faced by disenfranchised groups represented as casually related to an unjust society? Are the reasons for poverty and oppression explained, or are they accepted as inevitable? Does the story line encourage passive acceptance or active resistance? Is a particular problem that is faced by a person of color resolved through the benevolent intervention of a White person?

Role of Women

Are the achievements of girls and women based on their own initiative and intelligence, or are they due to their physical attractiveness or relationship to boys or men? Are sex roles incidental or critical to characterization and plot? Could the same story be told if the gender roles were reversed?

3. LOOK AT THE LIFESTYLES

Are people of color and their settings depicted in such a way that they contrast unfavorably with the unstated norm of White, middle-class suburbia? If the group in question is depicted as "different," are negative value judgments implied? Are people of color depicted exclusively in ghettos, barrios, or migrant camps? If the illustrations and text attempt to depict another culture, do they go beyond oversimplifications and offer genuine insights into another lifestyle? Look for inaccuracy and inappropriateness in the depiction of other cultures. Watch for instances of the "quaint-natives-in-costume" syndrome (most noticeable in areas such as clothing and custom, but extending to behavior and personality traits as well).

4. WEIGH THE RELATIONSHIPS BETWEEN PEOPLE

Do the Whites in the story possess the power, take leadership, and make important decisions? Do people of color and females function in essentially supporting, subservient roles?

How are family relationships depicted? In Black families, is the mother always dominant? Is the father always absent? In Latino families, are there always lots of children? Does the family live in close quarters? If a family is separated, are societal conditions—unemployment, poverty—cited among the reasons for separation?

5. NOTE THE HEROES AND HEROINES

For many years, books showed only "safe" heroes and heroines of color—those who avoided serious conflict with the White establishment of their time. People of color today are insisting on the right to define their own heroes and heroines based on their own concepts and struggles for justice.

When heroes and heroines of color do appear, are they admired for the same qualities that have made white heroes and heroines famous or because what they have done has benefited White people? Ask this question: Whose interests is a particular hero or heroine really serving?

The interests of the hero or heroine's own people? Or the interests of White people?

6. CONSIDER THE EFFECTS ON A CHILD'S SELF-IMAGE

Are norms established that limit any child's aspirations and self-concepts? What effect can it have on children of color to be continuously bombarded with images of the color white as the ultimate in beauty, cleanliness, and virtue and the color black as evil, dirty, and menacing? Does the book reinforce or counteract positive associations with the color white and negative associations with the color black?

What happens to a girl's self-image when she reads that boys perform all of the brave and important deeds? What about a girl's self-esteem if she is not "fair" of skin and slim of body?

In a particular story, is there one or more persons with whom a child of color can readily identify to a positive and constructive end?

7. CONSIDER THE AUTHOR'S OR ILLUSTRATOR'S BACKGROUND

Analyze the biographical information on the jacket flap or the back of the book. If a story deals with a theme associated with people of color, what qualifies the author or illustrator to deal with the subject? If the author and illustrator are not from the traditionally marginalized group being written about, is there anything in their background that would specifically recommend them as creators of this book?

8. CHECK OUT THE AUTHOR'S PERSPECTIVE

No author can be entirely objective. All authors write from a cultural as well as from a personal context. Children's books in the past have traditionally come from authors who were White and middle-class, with one result being that a single ethnocentric perspective has dominated children's literature in the United States. With any book in question, read carefully to determine whether the direction of the author's perspective substantially weakens or strengthens the value of his or her written work. Is the perspective patriarchal or feminist? Is it solely Eurocentric, or do people of color's perspectives also surface?

9. WATCH FOR LOADED WORDS

A word is loaded when it has offensive overtones. Examples of loaded adjectives (usually racist) are "savage," "primitive," "conniving," "lazy," "superstitious," "treacherous," "wily," "crafty," "inscrutable," "docile," and "backward."

Look for sexist language and adjectives that exclude or in any way demean girls or women. Look for use of the male pronoun to refer to both males and females.

Although the generic use of the word "man" was accepted in the past, its use today is outmoded. The following examples show how sexist language can be avoided: ancestors instead of forefathers; chairperson instead of chairman; community instead of brotherhood; firefighters instead of firemen; manufactured instead of man-made; human family instead of family of man.

10. LOOK AT THE COPYRIGHT DATE

Book on themes associated with traditionally marginalized groups—usually hastily conceived—suddenly began appearing in the mid and late 1960s. There followed a growing number of "minority experience" books to meet the new market demand, but these books were still written by white authors, edited by White editors, and published by White publishers. They therefore reflected a White point of view. Not until the early 1970s did the children's book world begin to even remotely reflect the realities of a pluralistic society. The new direction resulted from the emergence of authors of color writing about their own experiences in an oppressive society. This promising direction has been reversing in the late 1970s. Nonsexist books, with rare exceptions, were not published before 1972 to 1974.

The copyright dates, therefore, can be a clue as to how likely the book is to be overtly racist or sexist, although a recent copyright date, of course, is no guarantee of a book's relevance or sensitivity. The copyright date only means the year the book was published. It usually takes two years—and often much more than that—from the time a manuscript is submitted to the publisher to the time it is actually printed and put on the market. This time lag meant very little in the past, but in a period of rapid change and new consciousness, when children's book publishing is attempting to be relevant, it is becoming increasingly significant.

Appendix E: Coretta Scott King Award Winners and Honor Books

The Coretta Scott King Award, an official award that is recognized by the American Library Association, was initiated by school librarian, Glyndon Greer, in 1969. While attending the American Library Association's annual conference, Mrs. Greer recruited school librarian Mabel McKissack and book publisher John Carroll. This group organized the Coretta Scott King Award. During the first year, four other professionals joined the founders. They were Harriet Brown; Beatrice James, president of the New Jersey Library Association; Roger McDonough, New Jersey state librarian; and Ella Gaines Yates, assistant director, Montclair Public Library.

The award was originally designed to honor and encourage the aesthetic voice of the Black experience via literature and the graphic arts, including biographical, social, historical, and social history approaches by Black authors and illustrators. The criteria for selection include:

- The work must portray some aspect of the Black experience, past, present, or future.
- It must be written or illustrated by an African American.
- It must be published in the United States in the year preceding presentation of the award.
- It must meet established standards of quality writing for youth.
- It must be written for a youth audience.

- Particular attention will be paid to titles that seek to motivate readers to develop their own attitudes and behaviors as well as comprehend their personal responsibility as citizens in a pluralistic society.
- Illustrations should reflect established qualitative standards.

WINNERS AND HONOREES

1970
  Martin Luther King, Jr.: Man of Peace by Lillie Patterson

1971
  Black Troubador: Langston Hughes by Charlemae Rollins

1972
  17 Black Artists by Elton C. Fax

1973
  I Never Had It Made: The Autobiography of Jackie Robinson as told to Alfred Duckett

1974 Author Award Winner
  Ray Charles by Sharon Bell Mathis, ill. by George Ford

1974 Illustrator Award Winner
  Ray Charles, ill. by George Ford, text by Sharon Bell Mathis

1975 Author Award Winner
  The Legend of Africana by Dorothy Robinson

1975 Illustrator Award Winner
  no award

1976 Author Award Winner
  Duey's Tale by Pearl Bailey

1976 Illustrator Award Winner
  no award

1977 Author Award Winner
  The Story of Stevie Wonder by James Haskins

1977 Illustrator Award Winner
  no award

1978 Author Award Winner
Africa Dream by Eloise Greenfield

Honor Books
The Day When Animals Talked: Black Folk Tales and How They Came To Be by William J. Faulkner

Marvin and Tige by Frankcina Glass

Mary McLeod Bethune by Eloise Greenfield

Barbara Jordan by James Haskins

Coretta Scott King by Lillie Patterson

Portia: The Life of Portia Washington Pittman, the Daughter of Booker T. Washington by Ruth Ann Stewart

1978 Illustrator Award Winner
Africa Dream, ill. by Carole Bayard; text by Eloise Greenfield

1979 Author Award
Escape to Freedom by Ossie Davis

Honor Books
Benjamin Banneker by Lillie Patterson

I Have a Sister, My Sister is Deaf by Jeanne W. Peterson

Justice and Her Brothers by Virginia Hamilton

Skates of Uncle Richard by Carol Fenner

1979 Illustrator Award Winner
Something on My Mind, ill. by Tom Feelings; text by Nikki Grimes

1980 Author Award Winner
The Young Landlords by Walter Dean Myers

Honor Books
Movin' Up by Berry Gordy

Childtimes: A Three-Generation Memoir by Eloise Greenfield and Lessie Jones Little

Andrew Young: Young Man With a Mission by James Haskins

James Van Der Zee: The Picture Takin' Man by James Haskins

Let the Lion Eat Straw by Ellease Southerland

1980 Illustrator Award Winner
Cornrows, ill. by Carole Bayard; text by Camille Yarbrough

1981 Author Award Winner
This Life by Sidney Poitier

Honor Book
Don't Explain: A Song of Billie Holiday by Alexis DeVeaux

1981 Illustrator Award Winner
Beat the Story Drum, Pum-Pum by Ashley Bryan

Honor Books
Grandmama's Joy, ill. by Carole Bayard; text by Eloise Greenfield

Count on Your Fingers African Style, ill. by Jerry Pinkney; text by Claudia Zaslavsky

1982 Author Award Winner
Let the Circle Be Unbroken by Mildred D. Taylor

Honor Books
Rainbow Jordan by Alice Childress

Lou in the Limelight by Kristin Hunter

Mary: An Autobiography by Mary E. Mebane

1982 Illustrator Award Winner
Mother Crocodile: An Uncle Amadou Tale From Senegal, ill. by John Steptoe; text by Rosa Guy

Honor Book
Daydreamers, ill. by Tom Feelings; text by Eloise Greenfield

1983 Author Award Winner
Sweet Whispers, Brother Rush by Virginia Hamilton

Honor Book
This Strange New Feeling by Julius Lester

1983 Illustrator Award Winner
Black Child by Peter Mugabane

Honor Books
All the Colors of the Race, ill. by John Steptoe; text by Arnold Adoff

I'm Going To Sing: Black American Spirituals, ill. by Ashley Bryan

Just Us Women, ill. by Pat Cummings; text by Jeanette Caines

1984 Author Award Winner
Everett Anderson's Good-bye by Lucille Clifton

Special Citation
The Words of Martin Luther King, Jr. compiled by Coretta Scott King

Honor Books
The Magical Adventures of Pretty Pearl by Virginia Hamilton

Lena Horne by James Haskins

Bright Shadow by Joyce Carol Thomas

Because We Are by Mildred Pitts Walter

1984 Illustrator Award Winner
My Mama Needs Me, ill. by Pat Cummings; text by Mildred Pitts Walter

1985 Author Award Winner
Motown and Didi by Walter Dean Myers

Honor Books
Circle of Gold by Candy Dawson Boyd

A Little Love by Virginia Hamilton

1985 Illustrator Award Winner
no award

1986 Author Award Winner
The People Could Fly: American Black Folktales by Virginia Hamilton, ill. by Leo and Diane Dillon

Honor Books
Junius Over Far by Virginia Hamilton

Trouble's Child by Mildred Pitts Walter

1986 Illustrator Award Winner
The Patchwork Quilt, ill. by Jerry Pinkney; text by Valerie Fluornoy

Honor Book
The People Could Fly: American Black Folktales, ill. by Leo and Diane Dillon; text by Virginia Hamilton

1987 Author Award Winner
Justin and the Best Biscuits in the World by Mildred Pitts Walter

Honor Books
Lion and the Ostrich Chicks and Other African Folk Tales by Ashley Bryan

Which Way Freedom by Joyce Hansen

1987 Illustrator Award Winner
Half a Moon and One Whole Star, ill. by Jerry Pinkney; text by Crescent Dragonwagon

Honor Books
  Lion and the Ostrich Chicks and Other African Folk Tales by Ashley Bryan
  C.L.O.U.D.S. by Pat Cummings

1988 Author Award Winner
  The Friendship by Mildred D. Taylor

Honor Books
  An Enchanted Hair Tale by Alexis De Veaux
  The Tales of Uncle Remus: The Adventures of Brer Rabbit by Julius Lester

1988 Illustrator Award Winner
  Mufaro's Beautiful Daughters: An African Tale by John Steptoe

1989 Author Award Winner
  Fallen Angels by Walter Dean Myers

Honor Books
  A Thief in the Village and Other Stories by James Berry
  Anthony Burns: The Defeat and Triumph of a Fugitive Slave by Virginia Hamilton

1989 Illustrator Award Winner
  Mirandy and Brother Wind, ill. by Jerry Pinkney; text by Patricia McKissack

Honor Books
  Under the Sunday Tree, ill. by Amos Ferguson, text by Eloise Greenfield
  Storm in the Night, ill. by Pat Cummings; text by Mary Stolz

1990 Author Award Winner
  A Long Hard Journey: The Story of the Pullman Porter by Patricia C. and Frederick L. McKissack

Honor Books
  Nathaniel Talking by Eloise Greenfield, ill. by Jan Spivey Gilchrist
  The Bells of Christmas by Virginia Hamilton
  Martin Luther King Jr., and the Freedom Movement by Lillie Patterson

1990 Illustrator Award Winner
  Nathaniel Talking, ill. by Jan Spivey Gilchrist

Honor Book
  The Talking Eggs, ill. by Jerry Pinkney; text by Robert D. San Souci

1991 Author Award Winner
  The Road to Memphis by Mildred D. Taylor

Honor Books
 Black Dance in America by James Haskins

 When I Am Old With You by Angela Johnson

1991 Illustrator Award
 Aida. ill. by Leo and Diane Dillon; text by Leontyne Price

1992 Author Award Winner
 Now Is Your Time: The African American Struggle for Freedom by Walter Dean Myers

Honor Book
 Night on Neighborhood Street by Eloise Greenfield; ill. by Jan Spivey Gilchrist

1992 Illustrator Award Winner
 Tar Beach, ill. by Faith Ringgold

Honor Books
 All Night, All Day: A Child's First Book Of African American Spirituals, ill. and selected by Ashley Bryan

 Night on Neighborhood Street, ill. by Jan Spivey Gilchrist: text by Eloise Greenfield

1993 Author Award Winner
 Dark Thirty: Southern Tales of the Supernatural by Patricia McKissack

Honor Books
 Mississippi Challenge by Mildred Pitts Walter

 Sojourner Truth: Ain't I a Woman? by Patricia McKissack and Frederick L. McKissack

 Somewhere in the Darkness by Walter Dean Myers

1993 Illustrator Award Winner
 The Origin of Life on Earth: an African Creation Myth, ill. by Kathleen Atkins Wilson; retold by David A. Anderson/SANKOFA

Honor Books
 Little Eight John, ill. by Wil Clay; text by Jan Wahl

 Sukey and the Mermaid, ill. Brian Pinkney; text by Robert D. San Souci

 Working Cotton, ill. by Carole Bayard; text by Sherley Anne Williams

1994 Author Award Winner
 Toning the Sweep by Angela Johnson

Honor Books
>*Brown Honey in Broomwheat Tea* by Joyce Carol Thomas; ill. by Floyd Cooper
>
>*Malcolm X: By Any Means Necessary* by Walter Dean Myers

1994 Illustrator Award Winner
>*Souls Look Back in Wonder*, ill. by Tom Feelings; text ed. by Phyllis Fogelman

Honor Book
>*Brown Honey in Broomwheat Tea*, ill. by Floyd Cooper, text by Joyce Carol Thomas
>
>*Uncle Jed's Barbershop*, ill. by James Ransome; text by Margaree King Mitchell

1995 Author Award Winner
>*Christmas in the Big House, Christmas in the Quarters* by Patricia C. and Frederick L. McKissack

Honor Books
>*The Captive* by Joyce Hansen
>
>*I Hadn't Meant to Tell You This* by Jacqueline Woodson
>
>*Black Diamond: Story of the Negro Baseball League* by Patricia C. and Frederick L. McKissack

Illustrator Award Winner
>*The Creation*, ill. by James Ransome; text by James Weldon Johnson

Honor Books
>*The Singing Man*, ill. by Terea Shaffer; text by Angela Shelf Medearis
>
>*Meet Danitra Brown*, ill. by Floyd Cooper; text by Nikki Grimes

1996 Author Award Winner
>*Her Stories* by Virginia Hamilton

Honor Books
>*The Watsons Go To Birmingham* by Christopher Paul Curtis
>
>*Like Sisters on the Homefront* by Rita Williams-Garcia
>
>*From the Notebooks of Melanin Sun* by Jacqueline Woodson

1996 Illustrator Award Winner
>*The Middle Passage: White Ships Black Cargo* by Tom Feelings

Honor Books
>*Her Stories*, ill. by Leo and Diane Dillon; text by Virginia Hamilton
>
>*The Faithful Friend*, ill. by Brian Pinkney; text by Robert D. San Souci

1997 Author Award Winner
Slam by Walter Dean Myers

Honor Book
Rebels Against Slavery: American Slave Revolts by Patricia C. and Frederick L. McKissack

1997 Illustrator Award Winner
Minty: A Story of Young Harriet Tubman, ill. by Jerry Pinkney, text by Alan Schroeder

Honor Books
The Palm of My Heart: Poetry by African American Children, ill. by Gregorie Christie; ed. by David Adedjouma

Running the Road to ABC, ill. by Reynold Ruffins; text by Denize Lauture

Neeny Coming, Neeny Going, ill. Synthia Saint James; text by Karen English

1998 Author Award Winner
Forged by Fire by Sharon M. Draper

Honor Books
Bayard Rustin: Behind the Scenes of the Civil Rights Movement by James Haskins

I Thought My Soul Would Rise and Fly: The Diary of Patsy, a Freed Girl by Joyce Hansen

1998 Illustrator Award Winner
In Daddy's Arms I Am Tall: African Americans Celebrating Fathers, ill. by Javaka Steptoe

Honor Books
Ashley Bryan's ABC of African American Poetry by Ashley Bryan

Harlem, ill. Christopher Myers; text by Walter Dean Myers

The Hunterman and the Crocodile by Baba Wague Diakite

1999 Author Award Winner
Heaven by Angela Johnson

Honor Book
Jazmin's Notebook by Nikki Grimes

Breaking Ground, Breaking Silence: The Story of New York's African Burial Ground by Joyce Hansen and Gary MacGowan

The Other Side: Shorter Poems by Angela Johnson

1999 Illustrator Award Winner
  I See the Rhythm, ill. Michele Wood; text by Toyoni Igus

Honor Books
  I Have Heard of a Land, ill. by Floyd Cooper, text by Joyce Carol Thomas

  The Bat Boy and His Violin, ill. by E. B. Lewis, text by Gavin Curtis

  Duke Ellington: the Piano Prince and His Orchestra, ill. by Brian Pinkney; text by Andrea Davis Pinkney

Bibliography

American Association of University Women (AAUW) Educational Foundation (1992). *How schools shortchange girls: The AAUW report*. New York: Morrow & Company.

Anderson, R. C., Hiebert, E. H., Scott, J. A., and Wilkinson, I.A.G. (1985). *Becoming a nation of readers: The report of the Commission on Reading*. Washington, DC: The National Institute of Education.

Angelou, M. (1969). *I know why the caged bird sings*. New York: Bantam Books.

Au, K. H. (1993). *Literacy instruction in multicultural settings*. Fort Worth, TX: Harcourt Brace.

Au, K. H., Carroll, J. H., and Scheu, J. A. (1997). *Balanced literacy instruction: A Teacher's resource book*. Norwood, MA: Christopher-Gordon Publishers, Inc.

Banks, J. A. (1993, 1989). Approaches to multicultural curriculum reform. In J. A. Banks and C. A. McGee Banks (Eds.), *Multicultural education: Issues and perspectives* (pp. 195–214). Needham Heights, MA: Allyn and Bacon.

Banks, J. A. (1994, 1988, 1981). *Multiethnic education: Theory and practice*. Boston: Allyn and Bacon.

Berry, M. F., and Blassingame, J. W. (1982). *Long memory: The Black experience in America*. New York: Oxford University Press.

Breggin, P. R., and Breggin, G. R. (1998). *The war against children of color: Psychiatry targets inner city youth*. Monroe, ME: Common Courage Press.

Bullivant, B. (1993, 1989). Culture: Its nature and meaning for educators. In J. A. Banks and C. A. McGee Banks (Eds.), *Multicultural educa-*

tion: Issues and perspectives (pp. 29–47). Needham Heights, MA: Allyn and Bacon.

Comer, J. P., and Poussaint, A. F. (1992). *Raising Black children: Two leading psychiatrists confront the educational, social and emotional problems facing Black children.* New York: Plume.

Cunningham, A. E., and Stanovich, K. E. (1998). What reading does for the mind. *American Educator, 22* (1, 2), 8–15.

Derman-Sparks, L., and the A.B.C. Task Force (1989). *Anti-bias curriculum: Tools for empowering young children.* Washington, DC: National Association for the Education of Young Children.

Dillard, J. L. (1972). *Black English: Its history and usage in the United States.* New York: Vintage Books.

Douglass, F. (1993, 1881). *Life and times of Frederick Douglass.* New York: Gramercy Books.

Du Bois, W.E.B. (1969). *The souls of Black folk.* New York: Signet.

Ford, B. A. (1992). Multicultural education training for special educators working with African American youth. In F. Schultz (Ed.), *Annual editions: Multicultural education 95/96* (pp. 41–47). Guilford, CT: The Dushkin Publishing Group/Brown & Benchmark Publishers.

Foster, M. (1997). *Black teachers on teaching.* New York: The New Press.

Gardner, H. (1983). *Frames of mind: The theory of multiple intelligences.* New York: Basic Books.

Gay, G. (1993). Building cultural bridges: A bold proposal for teacher education. In F. Schultz (Ed.), *Annual editions: Multicultural education 95/96* (pp. 34–40). Guilford, CT: The Dushkin Publishing Group/Brown & Benchmark Publishers.

Giroux, H. (1987). Introduction: Literacy and the pedagogy of political empowerment. In P. Freire and D. Macedo (Eds.), *Literacy: Reading the word and the world* (pp. 1–27). Westport, CT: Bergin & Garvey.

Glenn-Paul, D. (1997). Toward a multicultural perspective. In V. J. Harris (Ed.), *Using multiethnic literature in the K–8 classroom.* Norwood, MA: Christopher-Gordon Publishers, Inc.

Gordon, B. M. (1995). Knowledge construction, competing critical theories, and education. In J. A. Banks and C.A.M. Banks (Eds.), *Handbook of research on multicultural education* (pp. 184–199). New York: Simon & Schuster Macmillan.

Grant, C. A,. and Tate, W. F. (1995). Multicultural education through the lens of the multicultural education research literature. In J. A. Banks and C.A.M. Banks (Eds.), *Handbook of research on multicultural education* (pp. 145–166). New York: Simon & Schuster Macmillan.

Graves, E. (1997). *How to succeed in business without being White: Straight talk on making it in America.* New York: HarperBusiness.

Graves, M. F., Juel, C., and Graves, B. B. (1998). *Teaching reading in the 21st century.* Boston: Allyn and Bacon.

Harris, V. J. (Ed.). (1992). *Teaching multicultural literature in grades K–8.* Norwood, MA: Christopher-Gordon Publishers, Inc.

Herrnstein, R., and Murray, C. (1994). *The bell curve: Intelligence and class structure in American life.* New York: Free Press.

Holden, G. W. (1997). *Parents and the dynamics of child rearing.* Boulder, CO: Westview Press.

hooks, b. (1994). *Teaching to transgress: Education as the practice of freedom.* New York: Routledge.

hooks, b. (1997). *Wounds of passion: A writing life.* New York: Henry Holt and Company.

Hopson, D. P., and D. S. Hopson (1990). *Different and wonderful: Raising Black children in a race-conscious society.* New York: Fireside.

Irvine, J. J. (1991). *Black students and school failure: Policies, practices, and prescriptions.* New York: Praeger Publishers.

Johnson, D. (1990). *Telling tales: The Pedagogy and promise of African American literature for youth.* Westport, CT: Greenwood Press.

Kozol, J. (1991). *Savage inequalities.* New York: HarperPerennial.

Lawrence, C. R. (1995). The word and the river: Pedagogy as scholarship as struggle. In K. Crenshaw, N. Gotanda, G. Peller, and K. Thomas (Eds.), *Critical race theory* (pp. 336–351). New York: The New Press.

Lee, C. D., and Slaughter-Defoe, D. T. (1995). Historical and sociocultural influences on African American education. In J. A. Banks and C.A.M. Banks (Eds.), *Handbook of research on multicultural education* (pp. 348–371). New York: Simon & Schuster Macmillan.

Malcolm X. (1965, 1964). *The autobiography of Malcolm X as told to Alex Haley.* New York: Ballantine Books.

Minami, M., and Ovando, C. (1995). Language issues in multicultural contexts. In J. A. Banks and C.A.M. Banks (Eds.), *Handbook of research on multicultural education* (pp. 427–444). New York: Macmillan.

Morrow, L. M. (1997). *Literacy development in the early years: Helping children read and write* (3rd ed.). Boston: Allyn and Bacon.

Nikuradse, T. (1996). *My mother had a dream: African-American women share their mothers' words of wisdom.* New York: Dutton.

Parks, G. (1997). Introduction. In A. Givens (Ed.), *Spirited minds: African American books for our sons and our brothers.* New York: W. W. Norton & Company, Inc.

Paul, D. G. (1997, Jan. 9). Misinformation abounds: Despite media's attitude, Ebonics decision makes sense. *The Bergen Record.*

Paul, D. G. (1998, April). How to raise a TV critic. *The Bergen Record's Parent Paper.*

Paul, D. G. (1998, March). Memories for a lifetime: How to write letters your child will cherish. *The Bergen Record's Parent Paper.*

Petty, W. T., Petty, D. C., and Salzer, R. T. (1994). *Experiences in language: Tools and techniques for language arts methods.* Needham Heights, MA: Allyn and Bacon.

Rodman, B. (1985). Teaching's "endangered species." *Education Week, 5,* 11–12.

Shannon, P. (1990). *The struggle to continue: Progressive reading instruction in the United States.* Portsmouth, NH: Heinemann.

Smitherman, G. (1977). *Talkin and testifyin: The language of Black America.* New York: Houghton Mifflin.

Spear-Swerling, L., and Sternberg, R. (1996). *Off track: When poor readers become "learning disabled."* Boulder, CO: Westview Press.

Strickland, D. S. (1998). *Teaching phonics today: A Primer for educators.* Newark, DE: International Reading Association.

Tatum, B. D. (1997). *Why are all the Black kids sitting together in the cafeteria?: And other conversations about race.* New York: Basic Books.

Taylor, D., and Dorsey-Gaines, C. (1988). *Growing up literate: Learning from inner-city families.* Portsmouth, NH: Heinemann.

Wellman, D. (1977). *Portraits of White racism.* Cambridge: Cambridge University Press.

Williams, S. W. (1991). Classroom use of African American language: Educational tool or social weapon? In C. E. Sleeter (Ed.), *Empowerment through multicultural education* (pp. 199–215). Albany: State University of New York Press.

Woodson, C. G. (1990, 1933). *The Mis-education of the Negro.* Trenton, NJ: Africa World Press, Inc.

Index

About the Author

DIERDRE GLENN PAUL is Associate Professor of Reading and Educational Media at Montclair State University, NJ.